My greatest strength as a consultant is to be ignorant and ask a few questions

Peter Drucke

Contents of this Expert Toolkit Bundle

1. Accelerated SWOT Analysis Tool

2. Benchmarking Assessment Template

3. Business Diagnostic Findings Template

4. Business Initiative Project Charter

5. Capability Gap Assessment Template

6. Cost-Benefit Assessment Framework

7. Customer Experience Design Framework

8. Data Collection Plan Template

9. Failure Mode Effects Analysis Template

10. Five Whys Analysis

11. Future State Process Change Framework

12. Hypothesis Capture Template

13. Initiative Prioritization Map

Contents of this Expert Toolkit Bundle

Accelerated SWOT Analysis

A simple, but powerful method for thinking through strategic choices taking into account market dynamics and capabilities

Accelerated SWOT Analysis – Overview

What is it

The Accelerated SWOT Method is a simple approach that matches corporate capabilities against market conditions to develop strategic choices. The technique uses a grid to present trends, strengths, weakness and strategic choices on a single panel. The method lends itself to a collaborative approach - taking into account organizational strengths and weaknesses, and market trends. At the end of the exercise you will have a set of strategic imperatives that the leadership team can understand and buy into.

When to use it

The Accelerated SWOT Method is best used when a fresh perspective is needed on trends market and how they line up against corporate capabilities. It is helpful in bringing alignment across a leadership team at the strategic level. It is also a great method for validating strategic programs against and overarching corporate strategy – and when time or resources do not permit the use of the more comprehensive SWOT analysis.

Why use it

The Accelerated SWOT helps to solve a variety of problems: Lack of clarity on key strategic imperatives; Lack of confidence that current strategic imperatives take into account current corporate strengths, weaknesses and market conditions; Lack of strategic alignment across the leadership team; Lack of creative thinking around strategic choices that are available to the organization.

Accelerated SWOT Analysis – Method

Step 3. Document the assessment of internal capabilities. Focus on the key capabilities that are seen as core strengths or weaknesses within the organization.

Step 1. Using existing information and stakeholder interviews, document the organization's corporate objectives. If performing the accelerated SWOT on a subset of the organization, use those objectives.

Step 4. With an eye on the Strategic Objectives captured in the top left box, brainstorm potential strategic choices for the organization. Take on each section (Offensive, Conversion, Utilization, Defensive) sequentially.

Step 2. Document the key trends that are relevant to the business unit, product, geography used in step 1. Focus on the most influential trends that create opportunities or threats.

Strategic Objectives	Strengths	Weaknesses
Opportunities	Offensive Strategies	Conversion Strategies
Threats	Utilization Strategies	Defensive Strategies

A more comprehensive "How to" guide for SWOT Analysis can be found on experttoolkit.com

Accelerated SWOT Analysis – Method

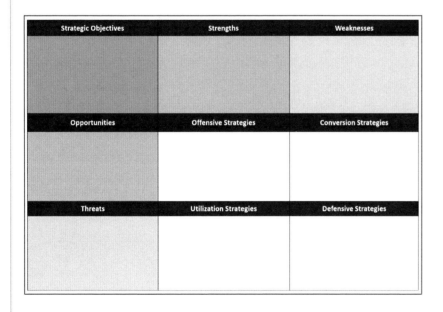

Offensive Strategies = Strengths plus Opportunity. Where can a market opportunity be exploited by leveraging a corporate strength.

Conversion Strategies = Weakness plus Opportunity. Where can market opportunities be leveraged to overcome a corporate weakness.

Utilization Strategies = Strength plus Threat. Where can a Strength be leveraged to overcome a market threat.

Defensive Strategies = Weakness plus Threat. What strategy can be employed to neutralize a weakness at the same time as mitigating a threat.

A more comprehensive "How to" guide for SWOT Analysis can be found on experttoolkit.com

Accelerated SWOT Analysis – Template

Strategic Objectives	Strengths	Weaknesses
Opportunities	**Offensive Strategies**	**Conversion Strategies**
Threats	**Utilization Strategies**	**Defensive Strategies**

Accelerated SWOT Analysis – Example

Strategic Objectives	Strengths	Weaknesses
• Drive domestic market share • Improve customer service • Improve operating margins • Expand into Eastern Europe • Lift shareholder value	1. Premium brand 2. Strong balance sheet 3. Offshore distribution centers 4. Retail sales footprint 5. R&D Capability	1. High operating cost base 2. Poor sales processes 3. Complex legacy systems 4. Unionized workforce 5. Limited big deal experience
Opportunities	**Offensive Strategies**	**Conversion Strategies**
1. Eastern Europe Conditions 2. Potential for alliances 3. Technology increasing demand 4. Sustainability agenda	1. (S1+O1+O2) Distribution alliance with XYX in Romania leveraging our brand 2. 3.	1. (W2+O1) Complete a process re-engineering exercise to support efficiency + market expansion 2. 3.
Threats	**Utilization Strategies**	**Defensive Strategies**
1. Increasing competition 2. Pricing pressure 3. Increasing deal complexity 4. Suppliers competing 5. Cyber security risks	1. Leverage balance sheet to purchase #3 competitor (S2+T1) 2. 3.	1. Conduct a cost optimisation program to improve margins and prepare for increasing price pressure (W1+T1+T2) 2. 3.

EXPERT TOOLKIT
— MAKE A GREATER IMPACT —

Benchmarking Assessment Template

A concise layout for comparing the performance
and practices of peer organizations as part of a
business diagnostic exercise

Benchmarking Assessment – Overview

What is it

The Benchmarking Assessment Template is a clear and simple framework for allowing organizations to be compared across a range of practices, performance measures, metrics or operational attributes in a visually appealing and easy-to-understand format. It can be easily tailored to suit the number of organizations or dimensions being compared, in addition to allowing other qualitative aspects to be highlighted as part of the read-out.

When to use it

The Benchmarking Assessment Template is best utilized as part of an analysis or diagnostics exercise where peer comparisons are being made across multiple organizations with the aim of highlighting areas of significant variation. It is particularly useful when needing to convey comparator variations to a senior executive audience or wide group stakeholders who need to be engaged and involved in action to address apparent performance or practice deficiencies.

Why use it

The Benchmarking Assessment Template is proven to be effective at conveying the critical information emanating from a peer comparison exercise. Its value comes through the ease with which direct comparisons between organizations can be made and, more importantly, communicated to a variety of audiences. Injecting peer comparison insights into a business analysis exercise can be extremely informative at highlighting the need for business transformation.

Benchmarking Assessment – Method (Option 1)

How you use it

Step 2. Capture the metrics, practices, measures in each area that are being assessed.

Step 3. For each metric or practice notate the relative performance and position of your organization compared to peer organizations.

Step 1. Capture the key dimensions or drivers that benchmarks, metrics, practices and comparators are being assessed.

Step 4. Use the correct symbols to notate the appropriate quartile positioning.

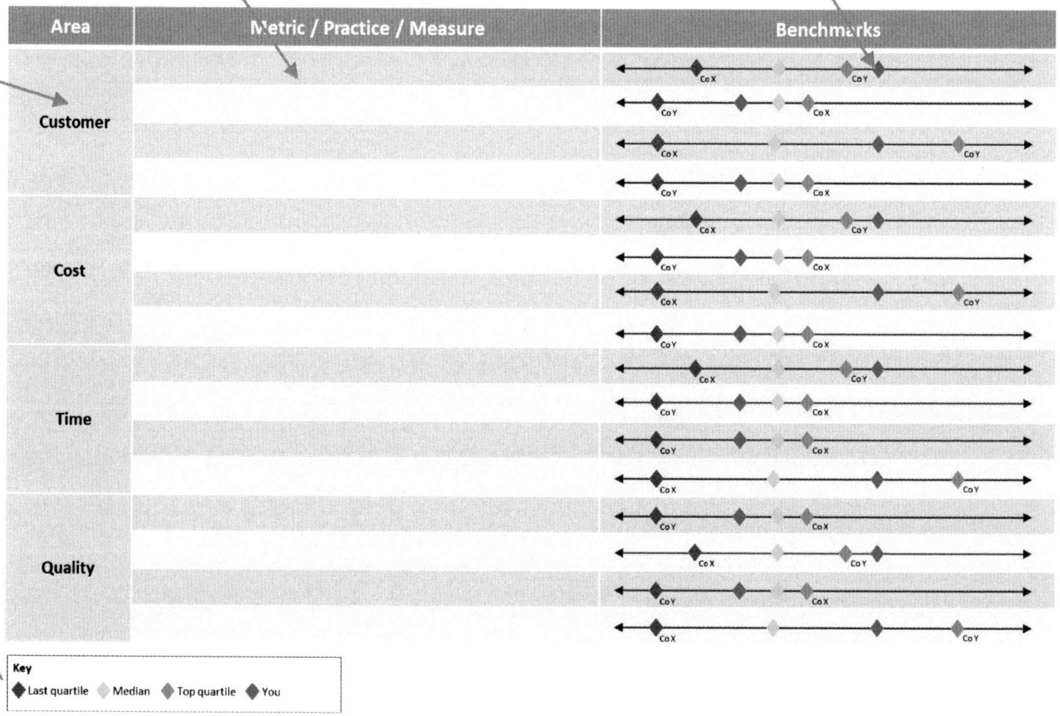

Area	Metric / Practice / Measure	Benchmarks
Customer		
Cost		
Time		
Quality		

Key
◆ Last quartile ◇ Median ◆ Top quartile ◆ You

Benchmarking Assessment – Template (Option 1)

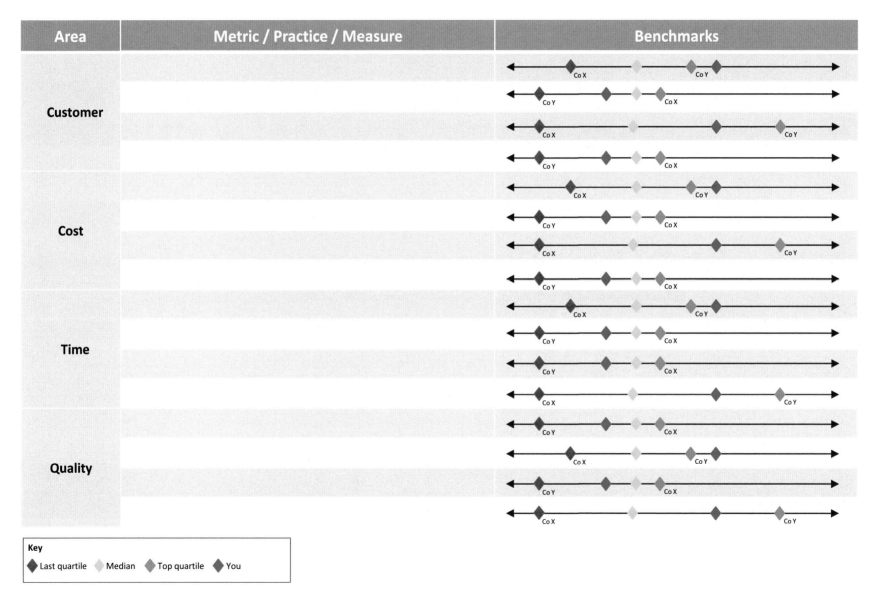

Benchmarking Assessment – Method (Option 2)

How you use it

Step 1. Capture the key dimensions or drivers that benchmarks and comparators are being assessed.

Step 2. Capture the metrics, practices, measures in each area that is being assessed.

Step 3. For each metric or practice, notate the relative performance and position of your organization compared to peer organizations.

Step 4. Capture any insights that emerge from the peer comparison and relative position across metrics and practices

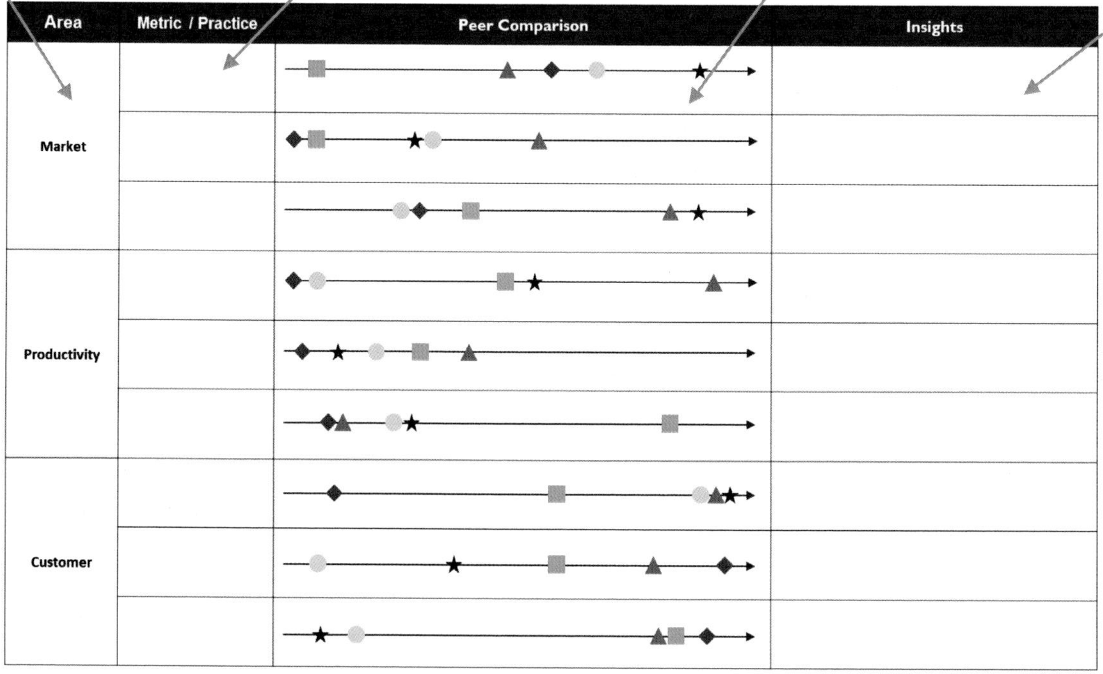

Area	Metric / Practice	Peer Comparison	Insights
Market			
Market			
Market			
Productivity			
Productivity			
Productivity			
Customer			
Customer			
Customer			

Benchmarking Assessment – Template (Option 2)

Area	Metric / Practice	Peer Comparison	Insights
Market			
Productivity			
Customer			

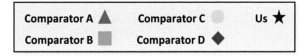

Comparator A ▲   Comparator C ●   Us ★
Comparator B ■   Comparator D ◆

EXPERT TOOLKIT
— MAKE A GREATER IMPACT —

Business Diagnostic Findings Template

A structured approach for presenting findings and observations from a business diagnostic exercise

Business Diagnostic Findings – Overview

What is it

The Business Diagnostic Findings Template is a proven framework for presenting the essential findings and observations from a business diagnostic phase. The format is highly adaptable and is particularly suited to presenting the summary outcomes from an analysis exercise to a group of key stakeholders. Two format options are presented here for selection by the business analyst. The template assumes that underlying analysis exists, providing sufficient evidence of the findings and these can be referenced if required.

When to use it

These templates should be used at the conclusion of a business analysis or diagnostic exercise when the key findings and observations are needing to be socialized with a stakeholder group. The template works for most varieties of analysis exercises – regardless of the focus being process, technology, organization, customer or other. The format for presenting the results works well as the segue into developing solution options or recommendations.

Why use it

The Business Diagnostic Findings Templates presented here are proven to work well with executive audience and are similar to those used by the leading management consultants reporting out findings to senior business executives. The format of the templates provide sufficient detail and are structured in a way to help the reader or audience understand the key facts and insights easily and therefore make informed decisions.

Business Diagnostic Findings – Method (Option 1)

How you use it

Step 1. Describe each focus area of the analysis exercise that has been conducted. This could be product, business unit, service type, systems – or any logical grouping that aligns with the approach and objectives of the exercise.

Step 2. Summarize the findings or observations for each focus area.

Step 3. Describe the likely impact of each finding.

Step 4. Outline potential solutions that could be adopted to counter the negative findings.

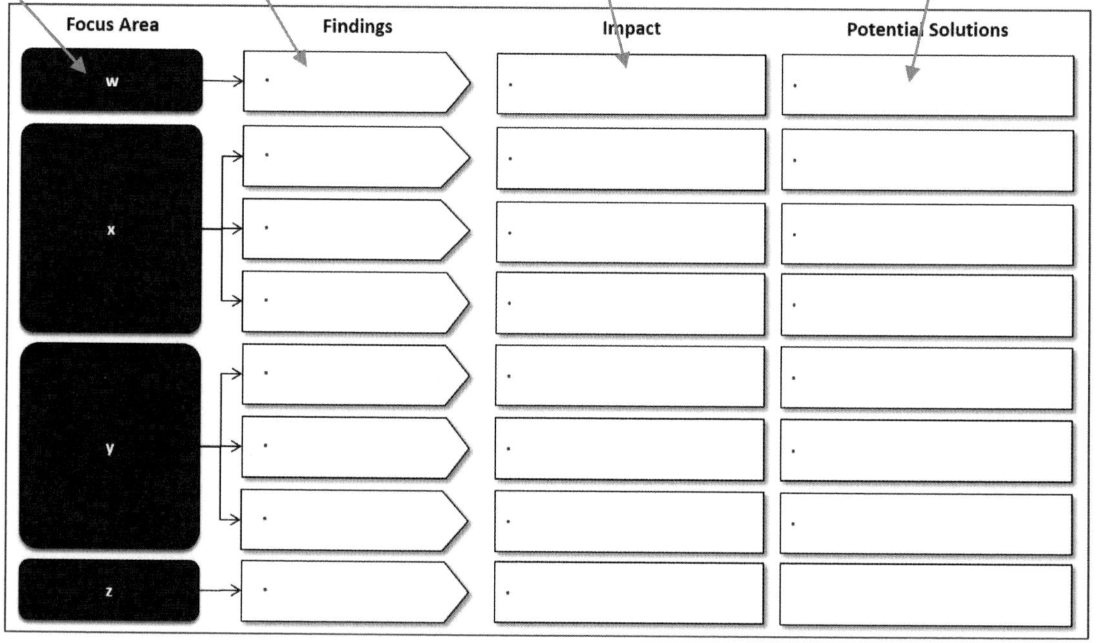

Focus Area	Findings	Impact	Potential Solutions
w	.	.	.
x	.	.	.
	.	.	.
	.	.	.
y	.	.	.
	.	.	.
	.	.	.
z	.	.	

Business Diagnostic Findings – Template (Option 1)

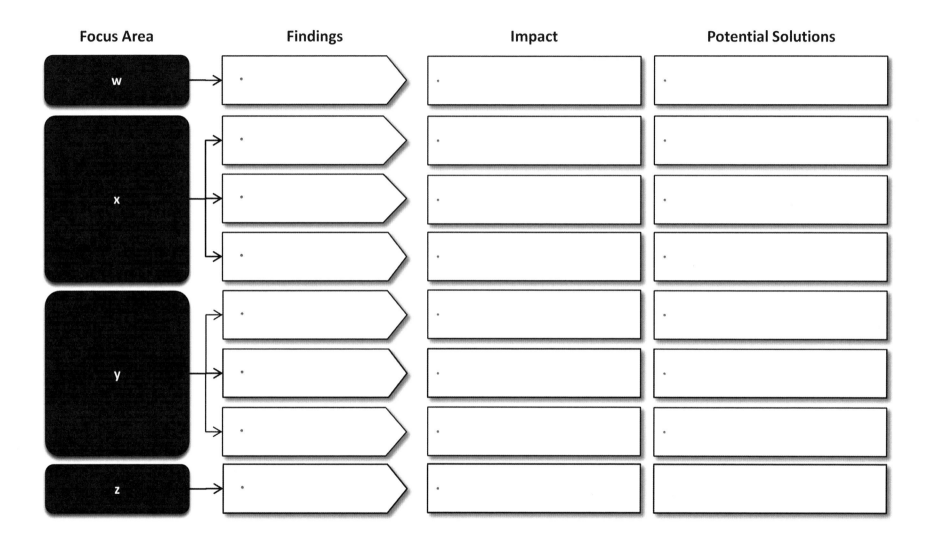

Focus Area	Findings	Impact	Potential Solutions
w			
x			
y			
z			

Business Diagnostic Findings – Method (Option 2)

How you use it

Step 2. Provide data, an example or other information as supporting evidence of the finding.

Step 3. Describe the known and potential impacts to the business caused by the finding.

Step 4. Use a key or legend to notate each finding, indicating which organizational dimension is impacted by the finding

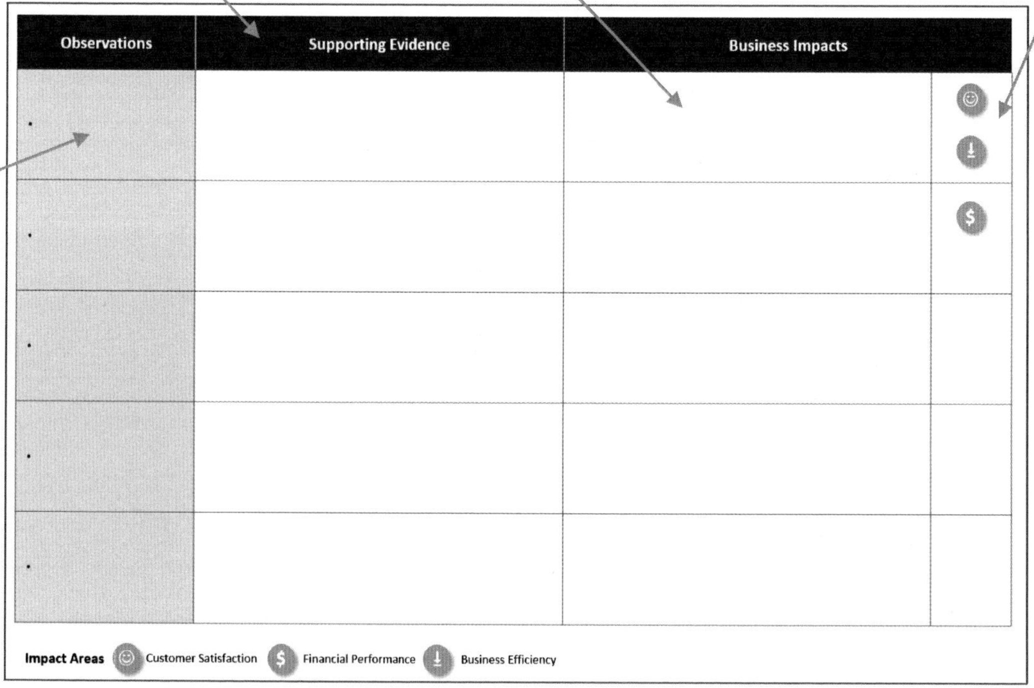

Step 1. Describe each observation or finding from the analysis exercise.

Observations	Supporting Evidence	Business Impacts	
.			☺
			⬇
.			$
.			
.			
.			

Impact Areas ☺ Customer Satisfaction $ Financial Performance   ⬇ Business Efficiency

Business Diagnostic Findings – Template (Option 2)

Observations	Supporting Evidence	Business Impacts	
•			☺ ↓
•			$
•			
•			
•			

Impact Areas Customer Satisfaction Financial Performance ↓ Business Efficiency

The Business Analysis Toolkit

EXPERT TOOLKIT
—— MAKE A GREATER IMPACT ——

Business Initiative Project Charter

A simple, clear, proven and customizable template for the effective definition of a business improvement initiative

Business Initiative Charter – Overview

What is it

The Business Initiative Project Charter Template is a simple, "on a page" view for laying out the key elements of a business analysis or improvement initiative including scope, objectives, activities, deliverables, stakeholders, measures of success and critical success factors. These elements and structures is easily customized to suit the needs of the business environment or project.

When to use it

This Business Initiative Project Charter should be used at the beginning of a project to clearly outline the scope, objectives and work required to be delivered as part of the project. The template can be used with the project team members to ensure alignment and the "job to be done" and can also be used with project sponsorship or other stakeholders to seek buy-in and endorsement.

Why use it

Clarifying and agreeing the scope, mandate and work to be delivered of a business initiative is a critical first step to ensuring success. This template is simple, clear, proven and customizable facilitating the efficient and effective definition of any business improvement initiative.

Business Initiative Charter – Method

How you use it

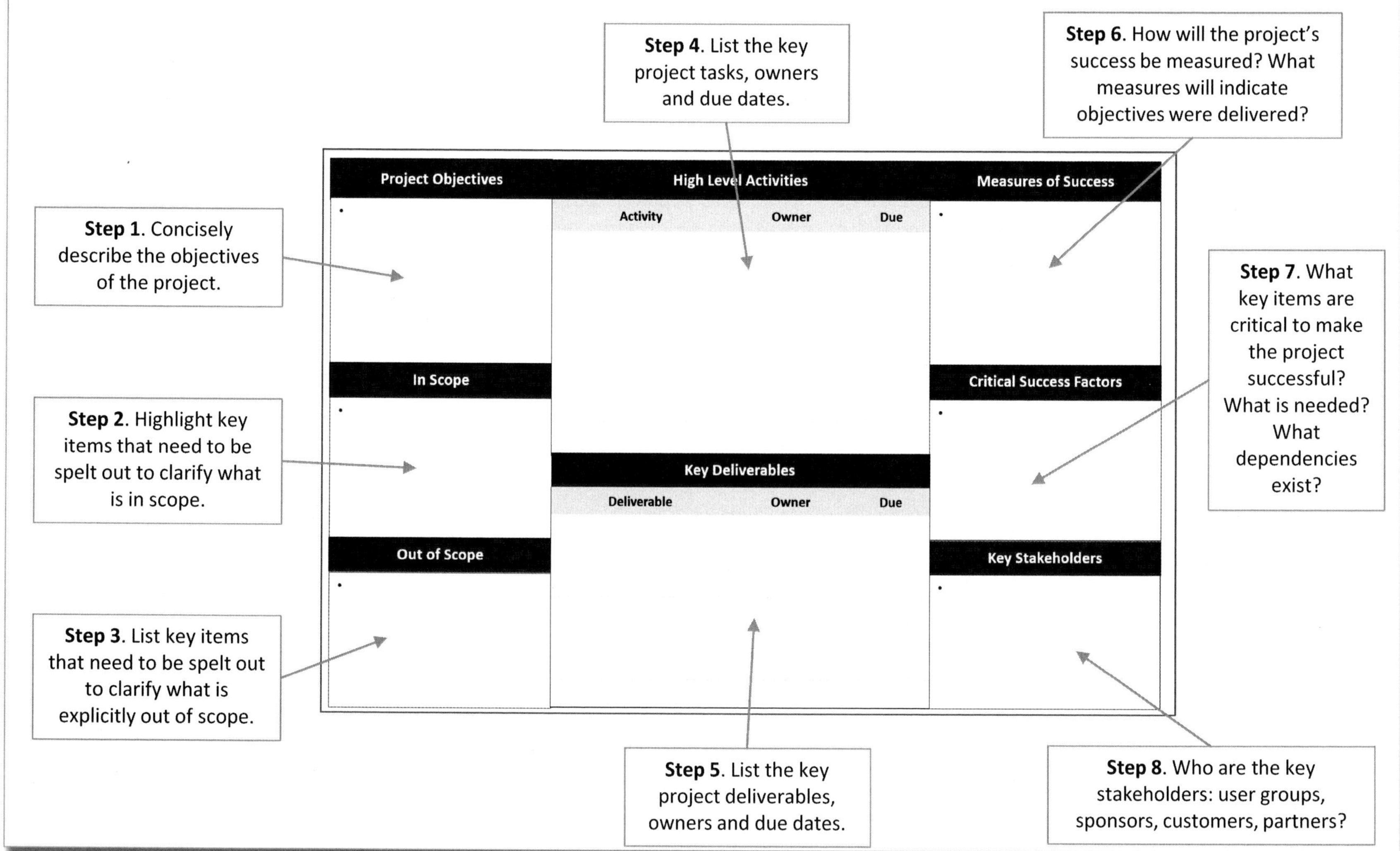

Step 1. Concisely describe the objectives of the project.
Step 2. Highlight key items that need to be spelt out to clarify what is in scope.
Step 3. List key items that need to be spelt out to clarify what is explicitly out of scope.
Step 4. List the key project tasks, owners and due dates.
Step 5. List the key project deliverables, owners and due dates.
Step 6. How will the project's success be measured? What measures will indicate objectives were delivered?
Step 7. What key items are critical to make the project successful? What is needed? What dependencies exist?
Step 8. Who are the key stakeholders: user groups, sponsors, customers, partners?
Project Objectives
In Scope
Out of Scope
High Level Activities
Activity
Owner
Due
Key Deliverables
Deliverable
Owner
Due
Measures of Success
Critical Success Factors
Key Stakeholders

Business Initiative Charter – Template

Project Objectives	High Level Activities			Measures of Success
•				•
	Activity	**Owner**	**Due**	

In Scope				**Critical Success Factors**
•				•

Out of Scope	Key Deliverables			Key Stakeholders
	Deliverable	**Owner**	**Due**	
•				•

Capability Gap Assessment

A structured framework for assessing the capabilities that exist within an organization.

Capability Gap Assessment – Overview

What is it

The Capability Gap Assessment is a structured framework for analyzing the capabilities that exist within an organization and presenting this assessment in a clear and simple form. The template allows a business analyst to capture multiple organizational dimensions, assess current capabilities and then outline potential improvement strategies to address apparent capability gaps.

When to use it

The framework is ideally suited to be used at the conclusion of an assessment phase, where findings need to be presented and potential strategies tested with stakeholders. The framework can be applied at a broad organizational level, also at a team or business unit level. Typically, the business analyst will have more detailed analysis and workings in support of the findings presented in the summary framework (such as interview notes, five whys, root cause etc.)

Why use it

This framework is especially useful when conducting a business analysis exercise that requires consideration of the capabilities that exist within the organization. It is highly adaptable and can be applied to tangible and less tangible organizational capabilities and across a range of dimensions including process, technology, people, culture, controls, governance, leadership.

Capability Gap Assessment – Method

Step 2. Summarize the capabilities that are required in this organizational dimension for the business to accomplish its objectives.

Step 3. Summarize the current capabilities that exist within the organization in this area.

Step 4. Rate the current organizational capability for each dimension (High, Medium, Low)

Step 5. Identify and capture the potential strategies to lift the organizational capability from the current level to the required level.

Step 1. Capture the dimensions or organizational aspects that are being assessed.

Dimension	Required Capabilities	Existing Capabilities & Rating		Potential Strategies
Brand	• Must have....	Currently have....	H	• Investigate the option of...
Service			M	
Pricing			L	
Network			H	
Offering			L	
Cost			L	
Invoicing			M	
Suppliers			H	

Capability Gap Assessment – Template

Dimension	Required Capabilities	Existing Capabilities & Rating		Potential Strategies
Brand	• Must have….	• Currently have….	H	• Investigate the option of…
Service			M	
Pricing			L	
Network			H	
Offering			L	
Cost			L	
Invoicing			M	
Suppliers			H	

Cost Benefit Assessment Framework

A proven, simple and flexible model for evaluating the costs and benefits of business improvement initiatives

Cost Benefit Assessment Framework – Overview

What is it

The Cost-Benefit Assessment Framework is a proven and easily customizable model for evaluating the costs and benefits of business improvement initiatives. It allows a business analyst or project owner to summarize the key dimensions that need to be considered when evaluating the worthiness of potential business improvement initiatives. The structure can be tailored to suit the specific requirements of the business, however the layout presented here is considered best practice.

When to use it

The Cost-Benefit Assessment Framework should be used to objectively evaluate business improvement initiatives and socialize them with executive stakeholders for selection and endorsement. The framework is designed to be used at the conclusion of an "analysis and design" exercise where issues are known in-depth and potential improvement projects have been identified, assessed and scoped. It is typical that additional financial worksheets will be created to support the information presented in this framework.

Why use it

The Cost-Benefit Framework is flexible and proven to work across a range of industries, environments and business improvement portfolio types. It provides a concise and structured mechanism for outlining potential improvement initiatives and prioritizing them based on pre-defined objective criteria – such as cost, financial return, strategic alignment, customer advocacy impact and benefit accomplishment risk.

Cost Benefit Assessment Framework – Method

How you use it

Step 2: For each initiative, provide a qualitative rating of alignment to strategic objectives.

Step 3: For each initiative, identify the pain points that will be remediated.

Step 4: For each initiative, provide a qualitative rating for the extent the initiative will have a positive impact on customers.

Step 5: For each initiative, provide details of Cost (OpEx, CapEx) and benefits (OpEx, Revenue) over 1 and 3 years.

Step 6: For each initiative, indicate the confidence level in the benefits being achieved.

Step 1: List the business improvement initiatives being evaluated.

Initiative Name	Strategic Alignment	Pain Points Addressed	Positive Customer Impact	Estimated Costs				Estimated Benefits (3yr totals $m)		Confidence Level of Benefits
				Capex ($m)		Opex ($m)				
				1ST YEAR	3 YEARS	1ST YEAR	3 YEARS	OPEX	REVENUE	
Example Initiative Name	High	#1, #2	High	0	0	1.5	2	4	4	Moderate
Example Initiative Name	Medium	#11, #14	Medium	3	5	1	3	10	50	High
Example Initiative Name	Low	#10	Low	1	4	2	6	5	27	Very High
Total										

Step 7: Total the results in order to assess the overall improvement portfolio.

Cost Benefit Assessment Framework – Template

| Initiative Name | Strategic Alignment | Pain Points Addressed | Positive Customer Impact | Estimated Costs | | | | Estimated Benefits (3yr totals $m) | | Confidence Level of Benefits |
| | | | | Capex ($m) | | Opex ($m) | | | | |
				1ST YEAR	3 YEARS	1ST YEAR	3 YEARS	OPEX	REVENUE	
Example Initiative Name	High	#1, #2	High	0	0	1.5	2	4	4	Moderate
Example Initiative Name	Medium	#11, #14	Medium	3	5	1	3	10	50	High
Example Initiative Name	Low	#10	Low	1	4	2	6	5	27	Very High
			Total							

Customer Experience Design Framework

A proven, simple approach for outlining a customer experience vision and design for an organization

Customer Experience Design – Overview

What is it

The Customer Experience Design Framework is simple-to-use, but very effective framework at structuring analysis and design of customer experience improvement. It uses three components to drive analysis, "visioning" and discussion: 1. The aspirational customer experience; 2. The current customer experience; and 3. The experience delivered by competitors. Using this simple model, aligned to the core steps taken by a customer along their experience journey allows improvement to be targeted for greatest return.

When to use it

The Customer Experience Framework is best suited to a future-state design exercise that is concentrating on the customer experience vision and design of an organization. To be most effective, some level of analysis and insight on the current state and competitor experiences will be available. Using this information, a business analyst can then facilitate a group of stakeholders to design an aspirational customer experience and from there agree on where the maximum improvement effort is required.

Why use it

The power of this Customer Experience Design Framework comes through its simplicity and adaptability. It can be tailored to any customer experience journey, any level of detail and any number of customer journey steps. It is also very effective when used to engage stakeholders during a future state customer experience design or "visioning" exercise in addition to executive socialization discussions aimed at soliciting buy-in and endorsement for process improvement or transformation.

Customer Experience Design – Method

Step 1: Identify the process steps that customers move through. The framework can be used at the highest process level or used at lower level process steps (for example the steps to purchase). Add steps along the horizontal as required.

Step 2: For each process step, summarize the experience that is being targeted for delivery to the customer.

Step 4: Draw experience curves that represent your organization's delivered experience and the experienced delivered by your primary competitor.

Step 3: Summarize the key points that represent the experience provided to customers by your primary competitor.

	Customer Lifecycle Step 1 (e.g. Browse)	Customer Lifecycle Step 2 (e.g. Buy)	Customer Lifecycle Step 3 (e.g. Use)	Customer Lifecycle Step 4 (e.g. Pay)	Customer Lifecycle Step 5 (e.g. Renew)
Our Desired Experience					
Wow!					
Pleasure					
Easy					
Procedural					
Confusing					
Frustrating					
Competitor's Provided Experience					

Step 5: Use the identified gaps in the experience curves and commentary (Steps 2 and 3) to identify process areas requiring the greatest improvement based on the difference between the current experience, competitor's experience and the aspirational experience.

Customer Experience Design – Template

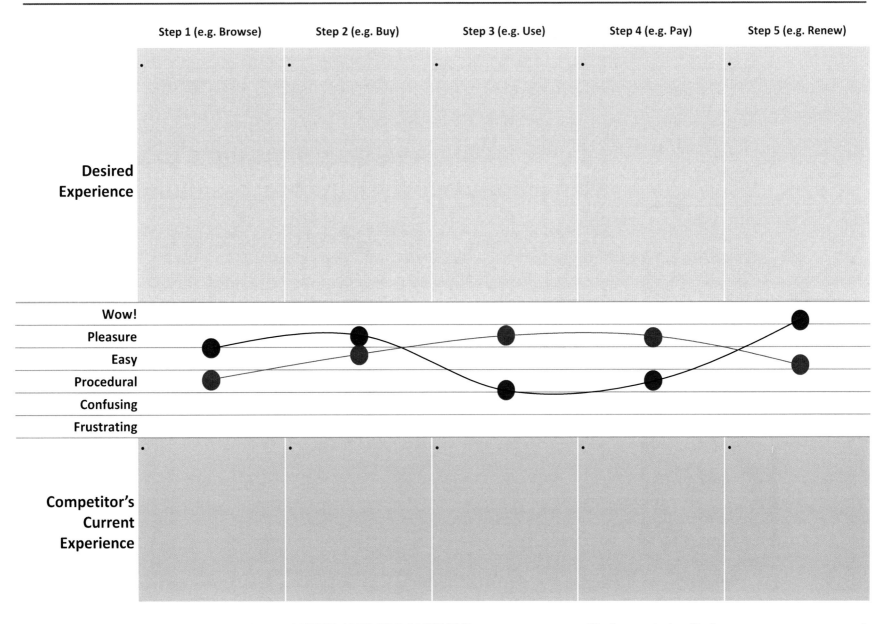

Data Collection Plan

A proven template for gathering operational data
in support of a business analysis exercise

Data Collection Plan – Overview

What is it

Business analysis initiatives need to begin with a clear understanding of the location, drivers, actors and implications of problems. To obtain this, it is essential the current state is understood intimately and accurately through data. Data is typically available from a range of sources, can be collected in a variety of methods, a variety of formats and can be obtained in different volumes. To gather the right data in the right format, in the right volumes and from the right sources is critical to have a good data collection plan.

When to use it

A Data Collection Plan should be used at the beginning of an analysis exercise that is endeavoring to understand the current state in order to get to heart of business problem drivers and root causes. Once the problem has been defined and initial hypotheses are being established, a data collection plan should be documented to outline and agree the data collection approach, volumes, sources, measurement volumes and time periods.

Why use it

A robust Data Collection Plan is critical to the success of any business analysis exercise. Clarifying the sources of data that will be gathered, analyzed, measured and used in a diagnostic is an important part of scoping, planning and approach definition. The Data Collection Plan template provided here is a proven structured approach for defining this plan.

Data Collection Plan – Method

Step 3. List the data, types and sources that need to be gathered to help answer the questions.

Step 4. For each data item, list the measurement approach, frequency, volume, sampling strategy, time period and recording method.

Step 1. Describe the problem statement – what is happening? What is being experienced? What business metrics are being impacted?

Step 2. List the key questions that need to be answered to understand the problem and its drivers.

Project Name: Data Collection Plan

Problem Statement:

Questions:

1.

2.

3.

Data			Approach				
Data	Type	Source	Measurement Approach	Frequency	Volume & Sampling Strategy	Time Period	How & Where to Record

Data Collection Plan – Template

Project Name: Data Collection Plan							

Problem Statement:

Questions:

1.

2.

3.

Data			Approach				
Data	Type	Source	Measurement Approach	Frequency	Volume & Sampling Strategy	Time Period	How & Where to Record

Data Collection Plan – Example

Project Name: Data Collection Plan							

Problem Statement: High volume of customer complaints being received in the contact center by customer using the RixbyPro home integration unit.

Questions:

1. Why are customers calling?

2. Are the complaints related to product, service, pricing?

3. Are their particular types of customers who are calling?

Data			Approach				
Data	**Type**	**Source**	**Measurement Approach**	**Frequency**	**Volume & Sampling Strategy**	**Time Period**	**How & Where to Record**
Customer Complaints	Call Recordings	Call Quality System	Listening and capturing salient data	Calls to be listened to over a 10 day period	Total of 400 call recordings	3 month period	Hills call center using the call quality playback system
Customer Purchase Experience	Customer Feedback	Live Survey Data	Customer Interviews upon store exit after product purchase	Every customer purchasing	Minimum of 400 store customer interviews	1 month	5 stores across 3 cities
Customer Returns	Forms	Returns Center Customer Forms	Gather customer product return forms and capture salient data	Every customer form	Minimum of 400 return forms	3 month	Springfield Returns Depot

Failure Mode Effects Analysis

A proven analysis method for identifying and preventing business process failures and errors

Failure Mode Effects Analysis – Overview

What is it

Failure Mode Effects Analysis (FMEA) is a method for analyzing potential ways in which a process could fail impacting process performance, output quality, customer satisfaction. FMEA works by using a consistent classification approach in which failures are prioritized based on severity, detectability and likelihood. Failure modes are errors or defects in a process, design, or item, especially those that affect the customer, and can be potential or actual. Effects analysis refers to the evaluation of the consequences of failures.

When to use it

FMEA is a useful method for identifying and analyzing the potential "break points" of a process. It helps ask the questions – "where could this process go wrong, how bad will it be when it goes wrong, how likely will we see it has gone wrong and be able to correct it". Using the objective assessment and scoring approach, FMEA can be used to focus improvement efforts in areas likely to cause greatest impact. FMEA is a valuable technique to utilize in any process analysis exercise where control and output quality is critical.

Why use it

A successful FMEA activity helps a business analysis team identify potential failure scenarios based on past experience, similar products or processes. This then enables improvements to be crafted that design those failures out of the process or system with the minimum of effort and resource expenditure, thereby reducing development time and costs. FMEA is widely used in a variety of industries and is applicable to product and service oriented processes.

Failure Mode Effects Analysis – Method

How you use it

Step 2.
Identify and capture the potential modes (methods) in which the process can fail.

Step 3.
Rank the severity or impact of a process failure (A)

Step 4.
Rank the likelihood or frequency of a process failure (B).

Step 5.
Rank the likelihood the failure *won't* be detected, controlled or prevented (C).

Step 1.
Capture the process steps or tasks.

Process Step	Failure Modes	Severity (A)	Frequency (B)	Detectability (C)	Risk Prioritization Number - RPN (A x B x C)

Step 6.
Calculate the Risk Prioritization Number (RPN) by multiplying A x B x C.

Step 7.
Rank the process failures by RPN and direct process improvement / remediation activity at those areas with the highest RPN.

Tables for A, B and C are shown on the next page

Failure Mode Effects Analysis – Method

How you use it

Step 3.
Severity (A)

Rating	Meaning
1	No effect
2	Very minor – only noticed by highly discriminating customers
3	Minor – noticed by the average customer but functionality not affected
4-6	Moderate – most customers are frustrated by the error and will complain
7-8	High – loss of primary function and customers likely to defect, cancel
9-10	Very High and Hazardous – inoperative, could result in critical error, injury or death

Step 4.
Frequency (B)

Rating	Meaning
1	No known occurrences on similar processes
2-3	Low – relatively few failures
4-6	Moderate – occasional process failures
7-8	High – repeated failures occur
9-10	Very-High – almost inevitable that failures will occur

Step 5.
Detectability (C)

Rating	Meaning
1	Certain – tests will detect fault
2	Almost certain fault will be detected
3	High likelihood fault will be detected and prevented
4-6	Moderate likelihood fault will be detected and prevented
7-8	Low – manual inspection required and high likelihood faults will be missed
9-10	Fault very likely to be passed on to customer

Failure Mode Effects Analysis – Template

Process Step	Failure Modes	Severity (A)	Frequency (B)	Detectability (C)	Risk Prioritization Number - RPN (A x B x C)

Five Whys Template

A structured and disciplined method for identifying drivers of business problems

Five Whys – Overview

What is it

The Five Whys Method is a disciplined, powerful technique for questioning a business performance situation in order to understand "why things are the way they are" to arrive at a true, underlying root cause – not a symptom. The name is derived by the principle of asking "why" at least five times to get to the real cause or driver for a business problem. The actual number of times "why" is asked will vary from situation to situation – but the goal is always to get to and true root cause of the problem experienced.

When to use it

The Five Whys Method has incredible versatility and facilitates a range of perspectives being gathered in a short time period through its inclusive nature. It is therefore very useful in situations where there is a high degree of time pressure associated with solving a business performance issue and there are a range of stakeholders with insights to be provided regarding the issue and its likely causes. It can be used in one-on-one settings (such as focused interviews) or in workshops involving multiple participants.

Why use it

The Five Whys is effective at getting to potential business problem drivers quickly. Although qualitative in nature, the structured questioning and probing combined with the collective knowledge of a range of stakeholders makes it particularly useful in discovering problem drivers quickly and then using the knowledge gathered during problem identification to begin solution ideation.

Five Whys – Method

How you use it

Step 1. Clearly describe the problem statement – what is happening? What is being experienced? What business metrics are being impacted?

Step 2. List the stakeholders that will be interviewed as part of the problem diagnosis.

Step 3. For each interviewee, capture the answers to each why. The first why box captures the answer to "why is this problem happening" (or similar). Each subsequent why box captures the answer of why the previous answer is happening.

Step 4. After each interviewee has been asked enough whys (3-5 recommended) some common themes should emerge for the underlying root cause.

Step 5. Based on the common theme root cause, brainstorm potential solutions or containment measures with the interviewees.

Problem Statement:

Interviewee	1st Why	2nd Why	3rd Why	4th Why	5th Why

Underlying Root Cause:

Potential Solution or Containment Measure:

A more comprehensive "How to" guide for the Five Whys can be found on experttoolkit.com

Five Whys – Template

Problem Statement:

Interviewee	1st Why	2nd Why	3rd Why	4th Why	5th Why

Underlying Root Cause:

Potential Solution or Containment Measure:

Future State Process Change Summary Template

A concise format for outlining the key changes and improvements required to optimize a business process

Future State Process Change Summary – Overview

What is it

The Future State Process Change Summary Template is complementary to the Process Issues Summary Template. It is a clean and structured method for highlighting proposed improvements to a process in addition to the corresponding initiatives that need to be initiated in order to implement the improvements.

When to use it

The Future State Process Change Summary should be used at the conclusion of a process analysis exercise to convey in a summary form the information necessary for stakeholders to understand the recommended improvements. The change summary should be supplemented by more detailed process analysis conducted by the business analysis, which should support the findings and recommendations.

Why use it

The Future State Process Change Summary is a proven, clear and logical format for conveying the changes and initiatives necessary for driving business process improvement. It works very well with a variety of stakeholders and is particularly useful with executive audiences who primarily need to know the summary of the recommendations requiring endorsement.

Future State Process Change Summary – Method

How you use it

Step 1. List the roles that are involved in supporting the future-state process.

Step 2. List the key tasks or process steps that are involved in delivering the future-state process.

Step 3. Describe in detail the changes that are proposed in the current process to implement the future process.

Step 4. Document the initiatives and fixes that need to be implemented in order to deliver the changes required of the future-state process..

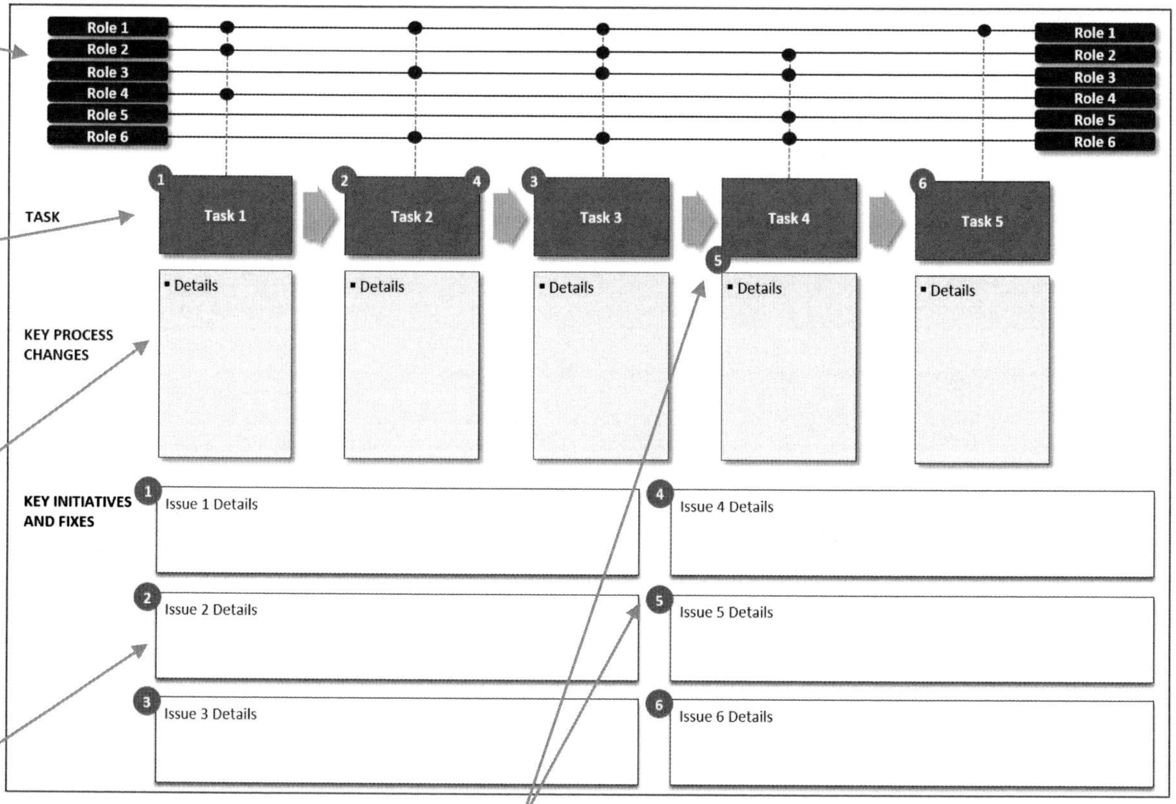

Step 5. Notate the fixes against the process steps that will be impacted by the fixes or improvement initiatives.

Role 1	Role 1
Role 2	Role 2
Role 3	Role 3
Role 4	Role 4
Role 5	Role 5
Role 6	Role 6

TASK

| 1 Task 1 | 2 Task 2 4 | 3 Task 3 | Task 4 | 6 Task 5 |

KEY PROCESS CHANGES

- Details
- Details
- Details
- Details
- Details

KEY INITIATIVES AND FIXES

1 Issue 1 Details	4 Issue 4 Details
2 Issue 2 Details	5 Issue 5 Details
3 Issue 3 Details	6 Issue 6 Details

Future State Process Change Summary – Template

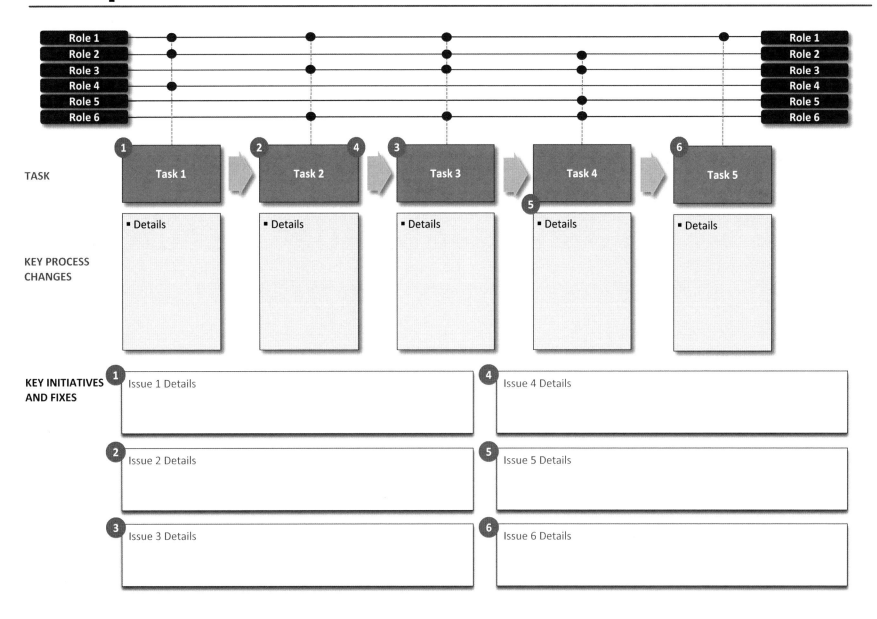

Hypothesis Capture Template

A structured framework for capturing hypotheses and driving fast-paced inductive business analysis

Hypothesis Capture – Overview

What is it

Hypotheses are developed during an inductive analysis (as compared to deductive analysis) exercise. Hypotheses are educated guesses that are then tested to assess if evidence confirms they are true or if they are false (dis-proven). Hypothesis-based business analysis facilitates fast-paced discovery and development of strategic choices. This Hypothesis-capture template is a proven and structured framework for capturing the necessary information associated with hypotheses as they are explored and tested.

When to use it

Hypotheses-based analysis is best used in circumstances where there is sufficient knowledge of the business environment and context to allow quality hypotheses to be developed and sufficient data and resources are available in order to test the hypotheses. When choosing to take a inductive-reasoning approach to a business analysis exercise, this template is useful in managing the various hypotheses and "lines of inquiry" that are evaluated.

Why use it

Hypotheses-based analysis is beneficial in facilitating an efficient and timely discovery of problems and opportunities by focusing the analysis effort in areas guided by the professional judgement of people closest to the subject matter. The alternative, deductive analysis, can be very time and effort intensive as it seeks to take a "bottom-up" approach of analyzing all available data to discover problems and opportunities for improvement.

Hypothesis Capture – Method

Step 3. Craft the hypothesis. The hypothesis is the item to be tested through analysis and should be developed based on professional judgement.

Step 4. List the lines of inquiry or data sources that need to be investigated and analyzed to confirm or refute the hypothesis.

Step 5. Following the analysis of the data sources and lines of inquiry, list the key findings or insights that were revealed.

Step 2. State the assertion which is an underlying belief or possible driver related to the problem. A good assertion leads to the development of a good quality hypotheses.

Step 1. Clearly describe the problem statement – what is happening? What is being experienced? What business metrics are being impacted?

Step 6. Document that conclusions as a result of the analysis. Was the hypothesis true or false? Is there work to be done to implement a measure to address the proven hypothesis or explore an alternate hypothesis?

Problem / Question	Assertions	Hypotheses	Data Sources / Lines of Inquiry	Findings / Insights	Conclusions

A more comprehensive "How to" guide for Hypotheses-based Analysis can be found on experttoolkit.com

Hypothesis Capture – Example

Problem / Question	Assertions	Hypotheses	Data Sources / Lines of Inquiry	Findings / Insights	Conclusions
Are we losing orders through poor quality sales processes? Sales orders and in-store stock are not reconciling.	There might be fraud occurring on the front-line which is causing the appearance of lost sales. This is a common problem in this industry and we have experienced it previously.	Absence of in-store controls are allowing sales orders to be manipulated resulting in stock loss and no corresponding order.	Order Data Stock Data Store Mystery Shopping Store Observations	At stores X, Y, Z stock levels and order levels are inconsistent by 3500 units (13%) for the month of April. We have large number of orders being processed to dummy accounts with no customer attached. These orders are concentrated amongst a finite set of sales reps.	The hypothesis is confirmed. There is an immediate need to implement proactive process and system controls to prevent fraudulent store sales.

Hypothesis Capture – Template

Problem / Question	Assertions	Hypotheses	Data Sources / Lines of Inquiry	Findings / Insights	Conclusions

EXPERT TOOLKIT
—— MAKE A GREATER IMPACT ——

Initiative Prioritization Map Template

A proven framework for categorizing and
prioritizing business improvement initiatives

Initiative Prioritization Map – Overview

What is it

The Initiative Prioritization Map is a structured framework for displaying, evaluating and prioritizing business improvement projects based on a simple two-by-two framework which generally considers a measure of the value of the initiative against a measure of the risk associated with delivering the initiative. Using this framework, initiatives can be categorized into different treatment groups to take forward.

When to use it

The Initiative Prioritization Map is ideally suited for use at the conclusion of an "Analysis & Design" project to evaluate potential improvement ideas, recommendations and initiatives. For effective use of the framework, initiatives should have already been identified and scoped to a sufficient level to know the relative business benefit and risk associated with delivery. The framework is also very useful for conveying a view of a prioritized improvement portfolio to senior executives for awareness and endorsement.

Why use it

The Initiative Prioritization Framework is simple, clear and easy to use – but powerful in its ability to stratify potential improvement initiatives into logical treatment categories to take forward. It is also proven to work well with senior executive business leaders for facilitating decision making on investments and garnering buy-in programs to take forward and those to defer or drop.

Initiative Prioritization Map – Method

How you use it

Step 2. Agree on the appropriate naming for each of the 4 quadrants based on the choices of the axes. Common naming is Strategic (top left), Quick Wins (top right), Drop (bottom left) and Evaluate (bottom right).

Step 3. Based on input from key stakeholders, plot the portfolio of initiatives on the prioritization map. Look for patterns and clustering of initiatives in certain areas. Agree to take initiatives forward based on the quadrant in which they fall.

Step 1. Confirm the dimensions of the matrix. The typical approach uses business value on the vertical and ease of delivery on the horizontal. Other options are cost to deliver, delivery risk, customer impact, pain point resolution.

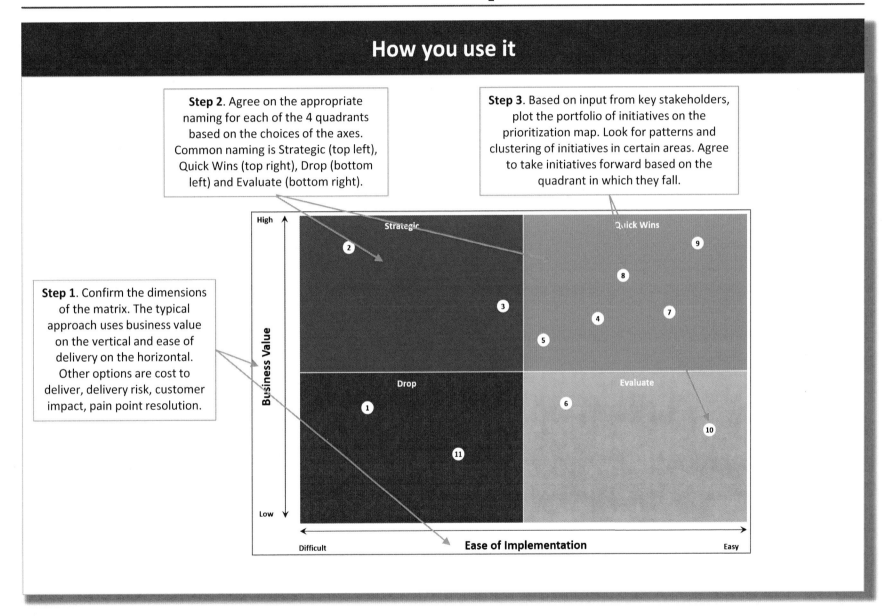

Initiative Prioritization Map – Template

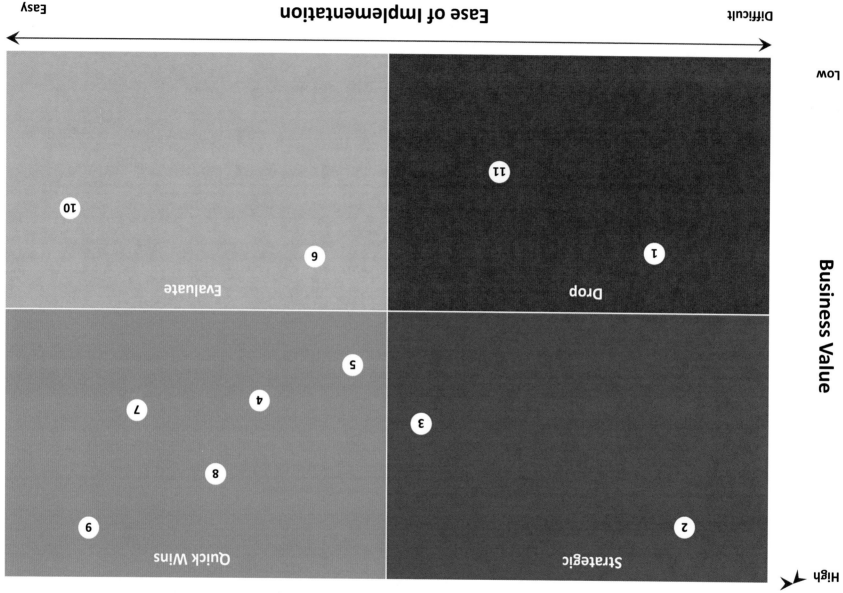

Ease of Implementation

Difficult   Easy

Business Value

Low   High

Drop — 11, 1

Evaluate — 10, 9

Strategic — 2, 3

Quick Wins — 6, 8, 7, 4, 5

The Jidoka Board Method

A structured, agile and disciplined method for identifying drivers of business process problems

Jidoka Board – Overview

What is it

Jidoka is a core pillar of lean thinking that requires management to develop processes that stop "production" immediately whenever an error or issue occurs. This stoppage then necessitates immediate error highlighting, resolution and error-proofing. At the heart of the philosophy is the principle that every user of a business process has the permission to stop a poorly operating process or raise issues that require remediation to improve performance. This makes Jidoka a powerful business analysis method.

When to use it

Jidoka has incredible versatility and facilitates a range of perspectives being gathered in a short time period through its inclusive nature. It is therefore very useful in situations where there is a high degree of time pressure associated with solving a business performance issue and there are a range of stakeholders with insights regarding issues and likely causes. It can be used in one-on-one settings or in workshops. It is also particularly powerful in an operational setting – facilitating continuous process improvement.

Why use it

The Jidoka Method is effective at getting to potential business problem drivers quickly. Although qualitative in nature, the structured questioning and probing combined with the collective knowledge of a range of stakeholders makes it particularly useful in discovering problem drivers quickly and then using the knowledge gathered during problem identification to begin solution ideation, development and implementation.

Jidoka Board – Method

How you use it

Step 1. As issues arise or ideas for doing things a better way these are captured on the board by the originator of the idea.

Step 2. Fellow team members cast votes on the ideas and issues according to their preferences. Voting can be done using colored stickers or simple notation of a vote with an 'x' or a line.

Step 3. Owners are allocated to each idea by the group. Owners take accountability for developing an action plan and implementing the solution.

Step 0. Using the template, create a large blank Jidoka Board with column headings and enough room to write in process issues or ideas. A laminated board can work with whiteboard markers for writing and colored stickers for voting.

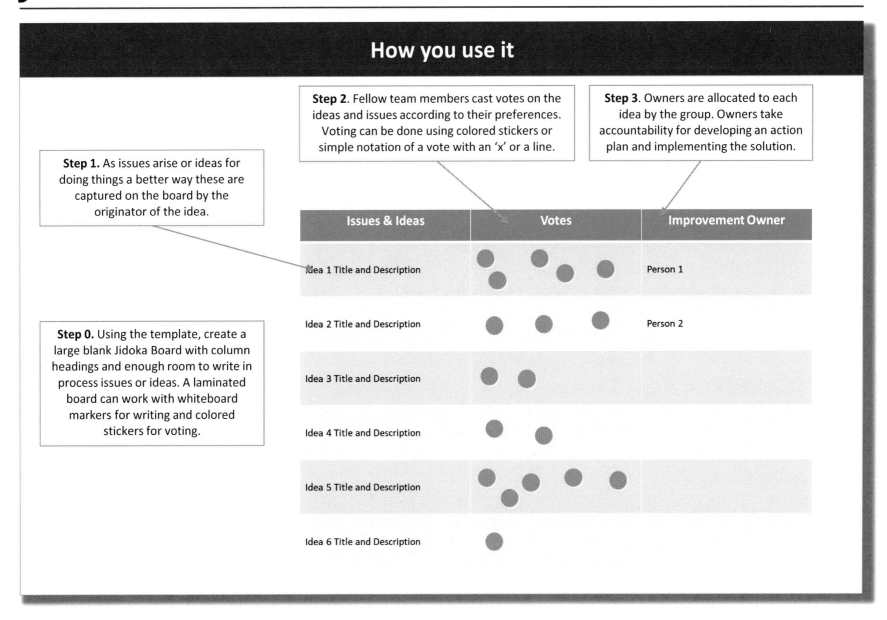

Issues & Ideas	Votes	Improvement Owner
Idea 1 Title and Description		Person 1
Idea 2 Title and Description		Person 2
Idea 3 Title and Description		
Idea 4 Title and Description		
Idea 5 Title and Description		
Idea 6 Title and Description		

Jidoka Board –Template

Issues & Ideas	Votes	Improvement Owner
Idea 1 Title and Description		Person 1
Idea 2 Title and Description		Person 2
Idea 3 Title and Description		
Idea 4 Title and Description		
Idea 5 Title and Description		
Idea 6 Title and Description		

Pain Point Analysis Template

A proven approach for representing, assessing and prioritizing the critical issues impacting a business process

Pain Point Analysis – Overview

What is it

Pain Point Analysis is a method for assessing the issues impacting the performance of a business process by considering the relative weighting of process issues across two dimensions. The analyst can choose the most relevant dimensions, however a typical combination is *impact* or *severity* combined with *volume* or *frequency*. An alternate to *volume / frequency* in some situations is *detectability*.

When to use it

Pain Point Analysis is a useful tool when assessing the current state performance of a business process and seeking to identify areas to focus remediation activity based on the likely return on effort. In other words, where will improvement time and resources reduce the most process pain. Effective use of the method is reliant on having stakeholders with suitable knowledge of process' current performance as well as the availability of relevant process performance data (e.g. volumes, error rates)

Why use it

Typically, processes will underperform across a range of areas – and a structured method for determining where to prioritize effort is critical to any process improvement exercise. Using Pain Point Analysis, a business analyst can guide an organization to agree on where maximum pain is being experienced and therefore where it is most essential to focus improvement effort and resources. Following Pain Point Analysis, Solution Ideation and Assessment are used to asses effort, feasibility and risk of solutions.

Pain Point Analysis – Method

How you use it

Step 3. Plot the known pain points on the matrix at the corresponding location. Solicit input from subject matter experts, process users and other stakeholders.

Step 4. Indicate with an arrow the expected trend for the pain point if no remediation activity is initiated. No arrow indicates no change expected.

Step 5. Capture the summary details of each of the pain points alongside the grid

Step 2. Use the grid – measured from low to high on each axes to plot each process pain point

Step 1. Decide on the most appropriate axes for the assessment. Here we use Occurrence vs Impact.

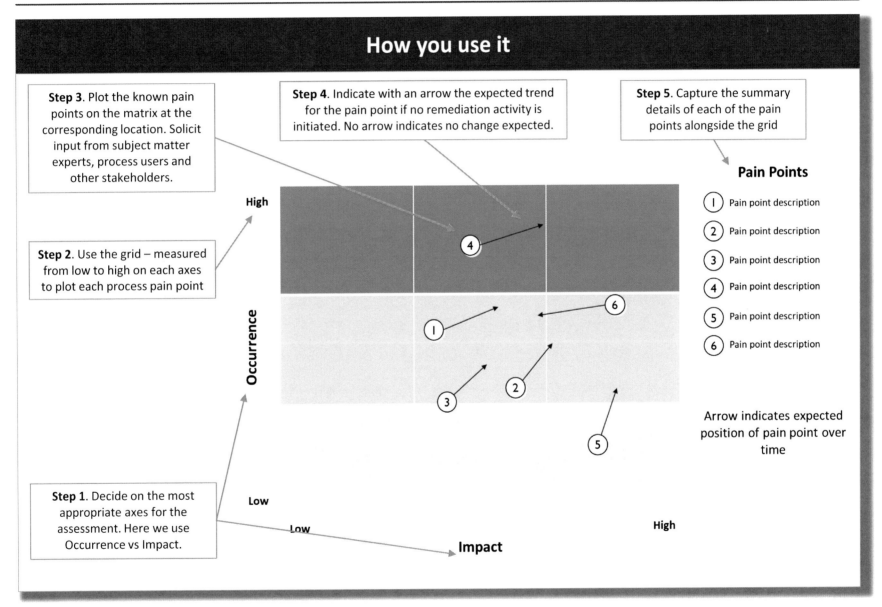

Pain Points

1. Pain point description
2. Pain point description
3. Pain point description
4. Pain point description
5. Pain point description
6. Pain point description

Arrow indicates expected position of pain point over time

Pain Point Analysis – Template

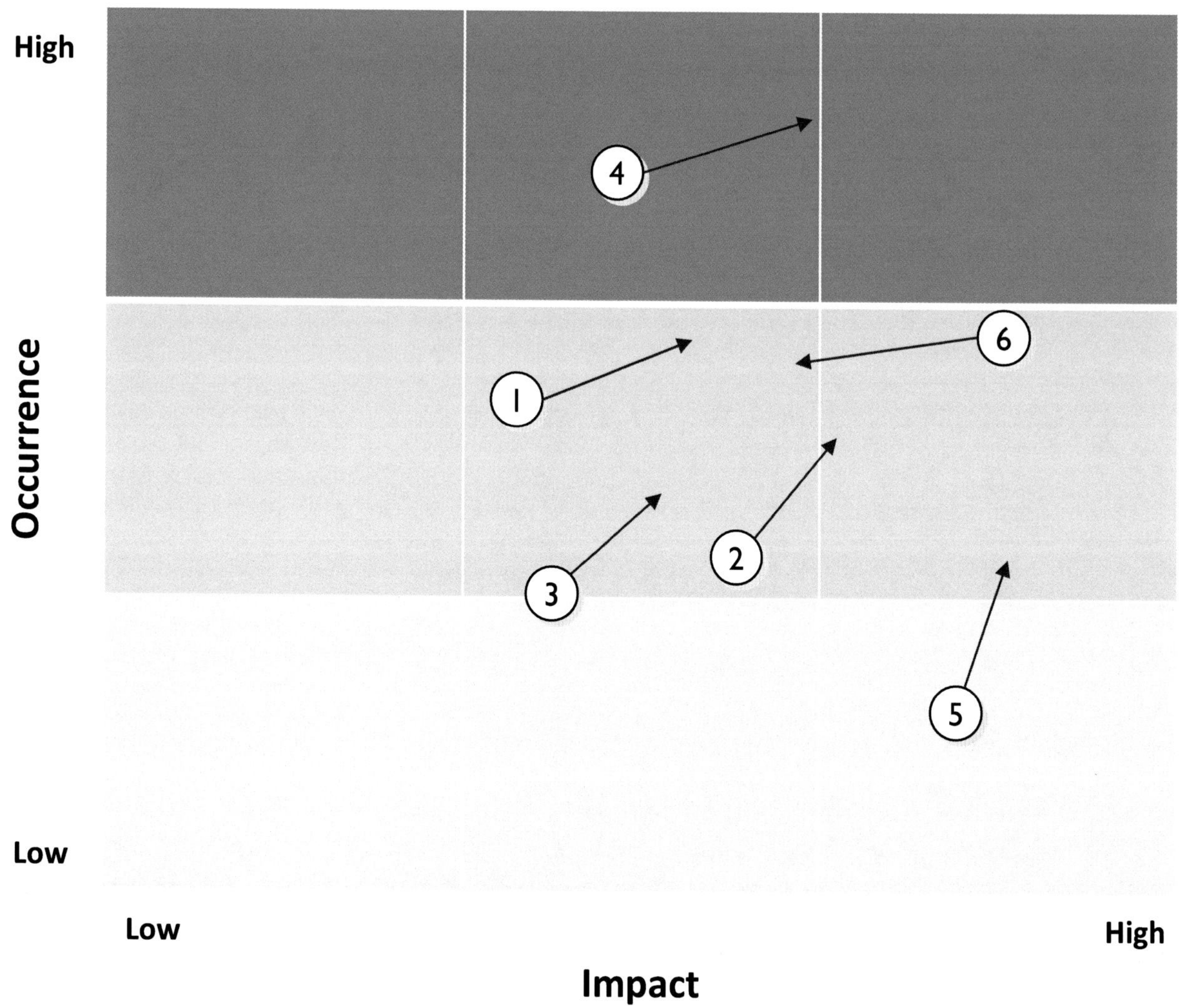

High

Occurrence

Low

Low

High

Impact

Pain Points

1. Pain point description
2. Pain point description
3. Pain point description
4. Pain point description
5. Pain point description
6. Pain point description

Arrow indicates expected position of pain point over time if no remedial action is taken

PEST Analysis Matrix Template

A proven method for assessing market trends and defining strategic choices to capitalize on those trends

PEST Analysis Matrix – Overview

What is it

The PEST Analysis Matrix is a framework for outlining the critical market trends impacting an organization, how they manifest as Opportunities or Threats and what Strategies could be adopted in order to capitalize on the market trends.

When to use it

The PEST Analysis Matrix Template should be used as part of strategic analysis exercise that adopts the PEST approach. The Template is helpful at synthesizing the key points pertinent to market trend analysis and in a format that can easily be included in a market assessment report. The Template is intended to be a summary information capture template that can be supplemented with more in-depth analysis worksheets where required.

Why use it

The PEST Analysis Matrix Template is concise and adaptable, providing a structured and logical mechanism for laying out the key market trends, impacts and strategies. It is a useful template for collating the essential information when conducting a strategic market analysis – this information can then, in turn, be summarized for communicating the most relevant trends and strategies to executive stakeholders.

PEST Analysis Matrix – Method

How you use it

Step 2. List each of the observed market trends from the PEST Analysis

Step 3. Summarize the evidence that exists to support the observation of the trend.

Step 4. Detail the Opportunities and Threats that are created by each Trend.

Step 5. Describe Strategic Hypotheses that could be adopted to capitalize on the trend.

Step 6. Describe the competitive advantage that would be gained by adopting the strategy.

Step 1. Provide each identified trend with a unique identifier.

#	Key Market Trends	Evidence or Observation of Trends	Implications		Strategic Hypotheses	Competitive Advantage Gained?
			Opportunities	Threats		

A more comprehensive "How to" guide for PEST Analysis can be found on experttoolkit.com

The Business Analysis Toolkit

PEST Analysis Matrix – Template

#	Key Market Trends	Evidence or Observation of Trends	Implications		Strategic Hypotheses	Competitive Advantage Gained?
			Opportunities	Threats		

EXPERT TOOLKIT
— MAKE A GREATER IMPACT —

Process Flow Analysis Template

A structured template for summarizing process
flow, key issues and improvement opportunities

Process Flow Analysis – Overview

What is it

The process flow analysis template is a proven, structured approach for outlining the flow of an end to end process in addition to its performance issues and opportunities for improvement. The template allows for all of the key attributes of a process to be captured (including inputs, outputs, steps, resources and description) in addition to the areas experience pain.

When to use it

This template is ideally suited for use at the conclusion of process analysis when key information is needing to be summarized and presented to an executive audience or other stakeholders. It is most applicable when the flow of a "left to right" process is relevant to the analysis and discussion. Note that the template includes 4 process flow steps, more can be added by using additional pages.

Why use it

This template is effective at conveying the key items relating to the process in terms of context, flow, attributes, issues and improvement opportunities. It is proven to work with executive audiences and a wide array of stakeholders needing to understand challenges facing an operational environment, the ideas for improvement and garnering support for transformation.

Process Flow Analysis – Method

How you use it

Step 1. Identify the input to each discrete step in the process.

Step 2. List the resources that are involved in supporting the process – these could be human.

Step 3. Name the step or task that is performed in this part of the process.

Step 4. Describe the step or task that is performed.

Step 5. Identify the outputs of the process step.

Step 6. Summarize the key issues that are experienced as part of this step in the process.

Step 7. Summarize the improvement opportunities that arise and would address the issues.

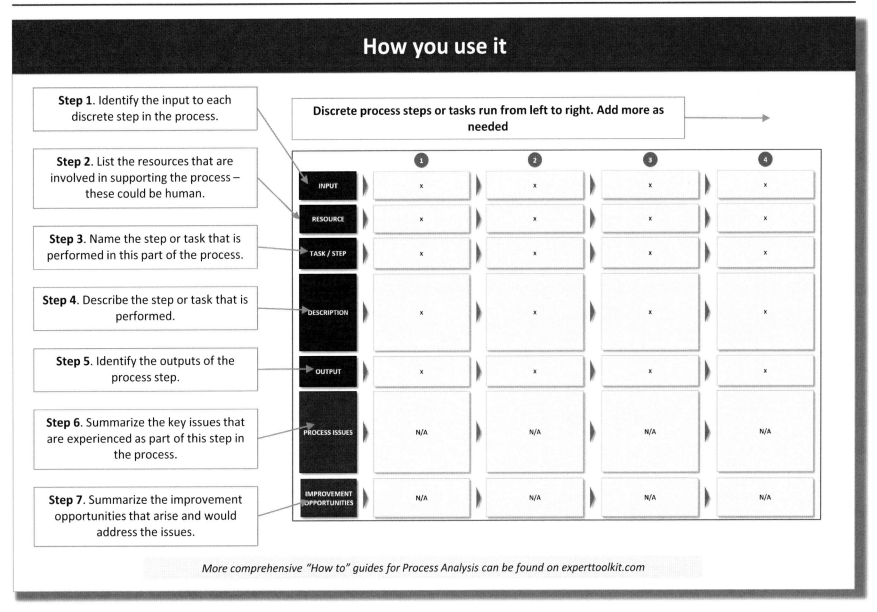

Discrete process steps or tasks run from left to right. Add more as needed →

	1	2	3	4
INPUT	x	x	x	x
RESOURCE	x	x	x	x
TASK / STEP	x	x	x	x
DESCRIPTION	x	x	x	x
OUTPUT	x	x	x	x
PROCESS ISSUES	N/A	N/A	N/A	N/A
IMPROVEMENT OPPORTUNITIES	N/A	N/A	N/A	N/A

More comprehensive "How to" guides for Process Analysis can be found on experttoolkit.com

The Business Analysis Toolkit

Process Flow Analysis – Template

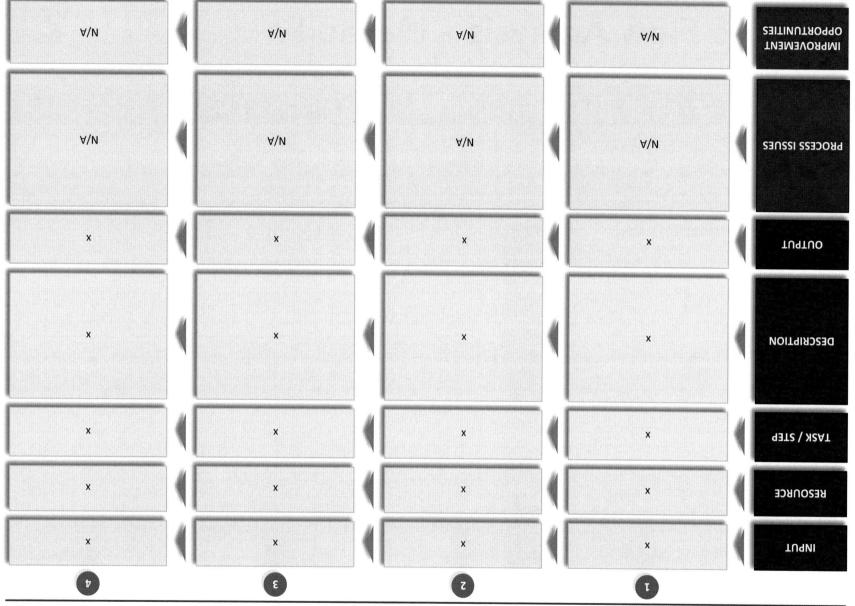

	INPUT	RESOURCE	TASK / STEP	DESCRIPTION	OUTPUT	PROCESS ISSUES	IMPROVEMENT OPPORTUNITIES
1	x	x	x	x	x	N/A	N/A
2	x	x	x	x	x	N/A	N/A
3	x	x	x	x	x	N/A	N/A
4	x	x	x	x	x	N/A	N/A

Process Issues Summary Template

A structured template for outlining key process
issues and challenges

Process Issues Summary – Overview

What is it

The process issues summary template is concise format for summarizing the key roles, steps and tasks that are involved in executing a process from end-to-end *and* the critical issues that are currently impacting the performance of the process.

When to use it

Use this template at the conclusion of a rigorous process analysis exercise when you are needing to summarize the key attributes of the process and the key issues that have been identified. It is ideally suited to conveying the key details to an executive audience or group of stakeholders who require some explanation of the process mechanics as well as the issues that are being encountered.

Why use it

This template is effective at conveying what needs to be conveyed in terms of process context and process issues. It is proven to work with executive audiences and a wide array of stakeholders needing to understand challenges facing an operational environment and therefore securing their support for improvement or transformation via process change.

Process Issues Summary – Method

Step 1. List the roles that are involved in supporting the process from end to end.

Step 2. List the key tasks or process steps that are involved in delivering the end to end process.

Step 3. Describe in detail the steps involved in performing the Task.

Step 4. Document the key issues that are observed or identified for each Task.

Step 5. Use numbered notations to link the issues to the process steps affected.

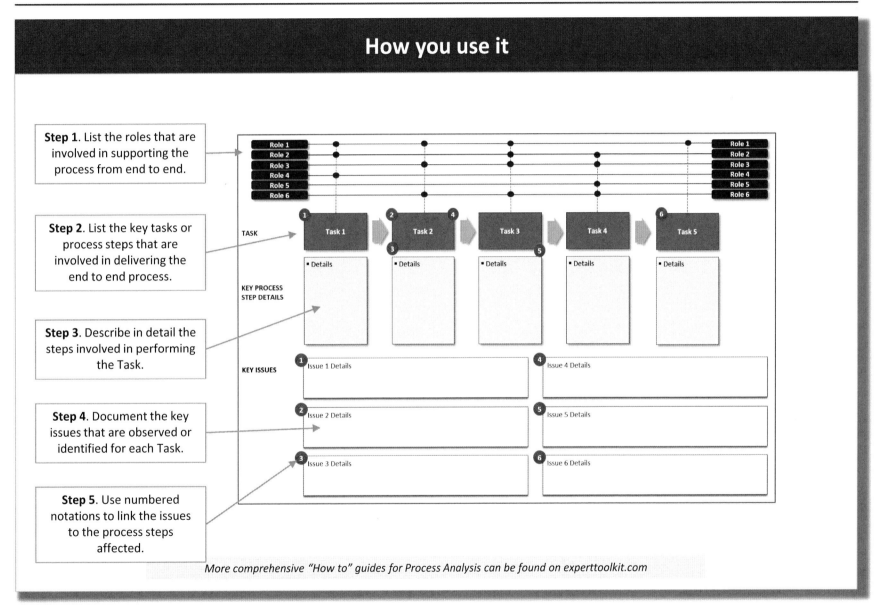

More comprehensive "How to" guides for Process Analysis can be found on experttoolkit.com

Process Issues Summary – Template

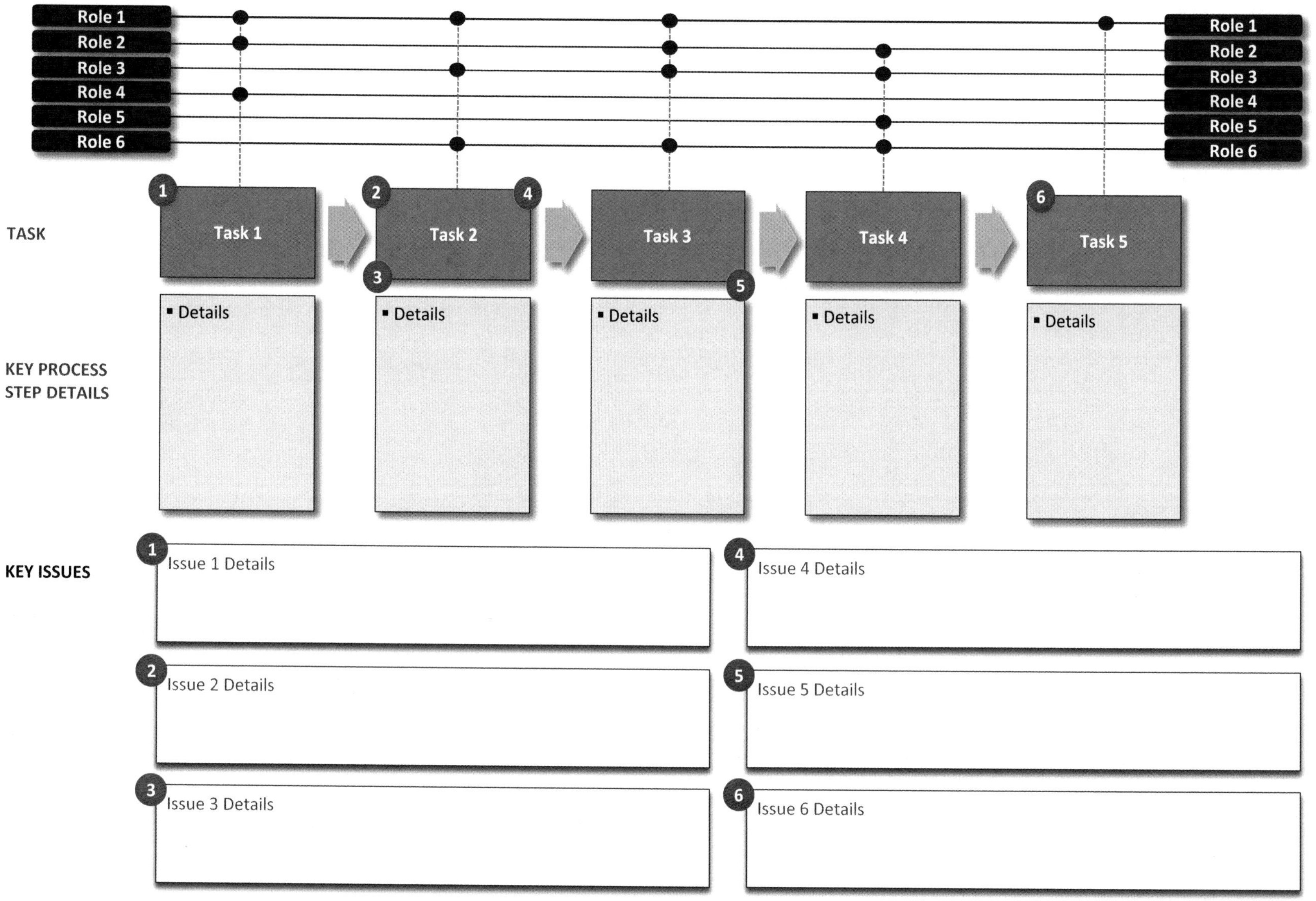

Role 1					Role 1
Role 2					Role 2
Role 3					Role 3
Role 4					Role 4
Role 5					Role 5
Role 6					Role 6

TASK

① Task 1	② ④ Task 2	Task 3	Task 4	⑥ Task 5
③		⑤		

KEY PROCESS STEP DETAILS

▪ Details	▪ Details	▪ Details	▪ Details	▪ Details

KEY ISSUES

① Issue 1 Details	④ Issue 4 Details

② Issue 2 Details	⑤ Issue 5 Details

③ Issue 3 Details	⑥ Issue 6 Details

Project Status Report

A concise and proven format for providing executive project status updates to key stakeholders

Project Status Report – Overview

What is it

The Project Status Report Template is a concise and clear layout for reporting regular status updates to sponsors and other stakeholders for a business analysis, improvement or transformation initiative.

When to use it

Use the template on a regular basis (weekly is recommended) during a business analysis, improvement or transformation project to provide updates and progress reports to sponsors and stakeholders.

Why use it

In any business initiative it is imperative to provide regular and concise updates to stakeholders with information on scope, activities, deliverables, risks, issues and progress. This template is proven to be effective at providing these updates.

Project Status Report – Method

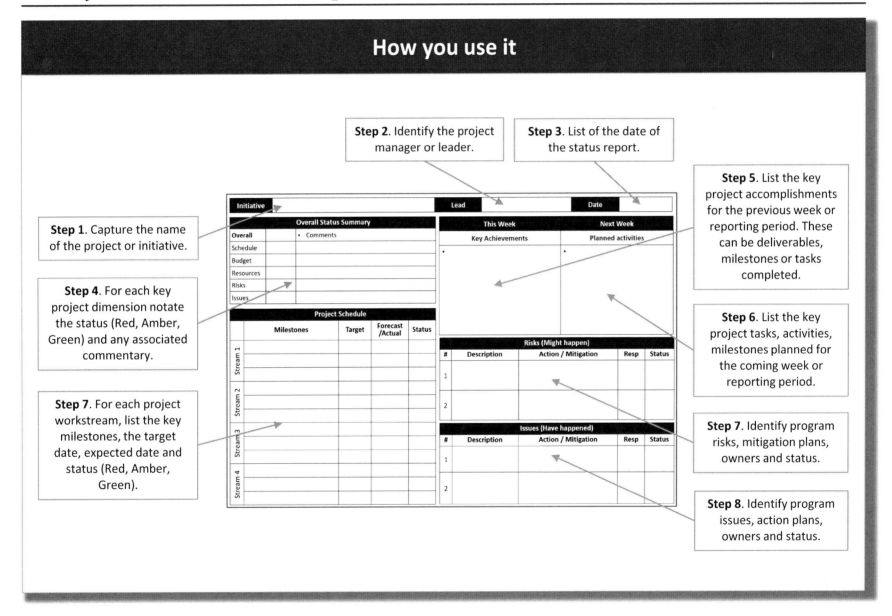

Step 2. Identify the project manager or leader.

Step 3. List of the date of the status report.

Step 5. List the key project accomplishments for the previous week or reporting period. These can be deliverables, milestones or tasks completed.

Step 1. Capture the name of the project or initiative.

Step 4. For each key project dimension notate the status (Red, Amber, Green) and any associated commentary.

Step 6. List the key project tasks, activities, milestones planned for the coming week or reporting period.

Step 7. For each project workstream, list the key milestones, the target date, expected date and status (Red, Amber, Green).

Step 7. Identify program risks, mitigation plans, owners and status.

Step 8. Identify program issues, action plans, owners and status.

Template elements

Initiative		Lead		Date	

Overall Status Summary

Overall	• Comments
Schedule	
Budget	
Resources	
Risks	
Issues	

Project Schedule

	Milestones	Target	Forecast /Actual	Status
Stream 1				
Stream 2				
Stream 3				
Stream 4				

This Week	Next Week
Key Achievements	Planned activities
•	•

Risks (Might happen)

#	Description	Action / Mitigation	Resp	Status
1				
2				

Issues (Have happened)

#	Description	Action / Mitigation	Resp	Status
1				
2				

Project Status Report – Template

Initiative		Lead		Date	

Overall Status Summary

Overall		• Comments
Schedule		
Budget		
Resources		
Risks		
Issues		

This Week / Next Week

	This Week	Next Week
	Key Achievements	Planned activities
	•	•

Project Schedule

	Milestones	Target	Forecast /Actual	Status
Stream 1				
Stream 2				
Stream 3				
Stream 4				

Risks (Might happen)

#	Description	Action / Mitigation	Resp	Status
1				
2				

Issues (Have happened)

#	Description	Action / Mitigation	Resp	Status
1				
2				

EXPERT TOOLKIT
— MAKE A GREATER IMPACT —

RACI Template

A structured business analysis technique for assessing and allocating workload across teams and individuals

RACI – Overview

What is it

RACI helps to clarify what activities & functions need to be done and who needs to do them. RACI development is a systematic process involving the identification of functions to be accomplished and clarification of roles and levels of participation for the activities. RACI is useful at clarifying the allocation of workload across teams and identifying inefficiencies in current workload allocation models. RACI development is meant to be collaborative – facilitating group involvement for design and buy-in.

When to use it

RACI is a useful tool in a number of business analysis and improvement scenarios: The distribution of workload across a team is sub-optimal; A team, function or business unit is reorganized and a method is needed to verify workload coverage and clarify responsibilities; Staffing changes necessitate team and individual workload coverage reviews; Functional procedures and accountabilities need clarifying and documenting.

Why use it

RACI is a very effective tool for identifying workload imbalances in teams. It can help to ensures that key functions and activities are not overlooked and that there is not surplus capacity. A RACI can help new team members rapidly identify their 'roles and responsibilities'. A RACI can provide a mechanism for discussion and resolving inter/intra team confusion around workload responsibilities. RACI is a simple way to document and communicate roles and responsibilities.

RACI – Method

Step 1. Determine the task, job or function that needs a RACI developed

Step 2. Determine and list the activities and roles involved in that task or job and the individuals involved

Step 3. For each activity, assign Accountability and the appropriate amount of R's, C's and I's to accomplish the task (see next page for definitions)

Step 4. Ensure all of the roles / individuals understand the requirements of them and are capable and committed to delivering

Step 5. Analyze RACI matrix for issues, inefficiencies and opportunities to improve (see 2 pages over for insights)

Functional Roles
Roles and positions assigned to complete an activity

Task Name						
Task 1						

Activities	Project Director	Team Leader	Technical Architect	Business Analyst	Process Lead	Finance Lead
Activity 1			R	A		
Activity 2	A/R		C	I	C	
Activity 3			I		A/R	C
Activity 4			R		A	
Activity 5	I		A		R	
Activity 6	A	I		R		C
Activity 7		A	C	R		I

A more comprehensive "How to" guide for the RACI can be found on experttoolkit.com

RACI – Method

How you use it

Step 3. Definitions

Responsible	• Someone who performs an activity and is responsible for the action being completed. "R"s can be shared across team members.
Accountable	• The individual who is ultimately accountable for the activity or decision – and includes yes/no and veto power. Only one "A" can be assigned to any activity/decision.
Consulted	• Individuals that need to be consulted prior to a final decision or before/after an activity is performed. "C" individuals participate in two-way communication.
Informed	• Individuals who needs to be informed after a decision or action is taken. "I" people receive one-way communication.

RACI – Method

Step 5. Insights

	What to look for	What it might mean
Horizontal	Lots of Rs	Too many people involved
	No Rs or As	Activity is not getting done or doesn't need doing
	More than one A	Uncertainty
	Lots of Cs	Too many people involved
	Lots of Is	Too many people being advised
Vertical	Lots of Rs	Too much work
	No empty spaces	Too much work or involvement
	No Rs or As	Activity is not required
	Too many As	Accountability not at the right level

The Business Analysis Toolkit

RACI – Template

Task / Function									
Activities / Decisions									

Root Cause Analysis Template

A proven business analysis method for getting to the heart of operational performance problems

Root Cause Analysis – Overview

What is it

The Fishbone Root Cause Analysis Method is a technique for analyzing business problems (symptoms) and drilling down to discover the true underlying root causes for the problem. It is a qualitative technique and relies on the participation of stakeholders who have knowledge of the operational environment and can therefore provide input into current problems and their potential causes.

When to use it

The fishbone method and tool is ideally suited to situations where brainstorming among a group of individuals is necessary to explore symptoms, possible root causes with the aim of prioritizing areas requiring further analysis, investigation, quantification and solution development. It is particularly useful in the development of hypotheses which can then be further tested with more rigorous, quantitative data analysis. It is particularly useful when combined with the 5 Whys Method.

Why use it

Root Cause Analysis digs down to the real problem - the 'root cause'. The process helps to break down what can appear to be an impossible-to-solve issue into smaller, more easily handled elements. It facilitates a structured discussion around possible root causes and allows targeted solution ideation to commence. It also helps to look beyond what may appear to be the issue, in order to identify the real driver of the problem.

Root Cause Analysis – Method

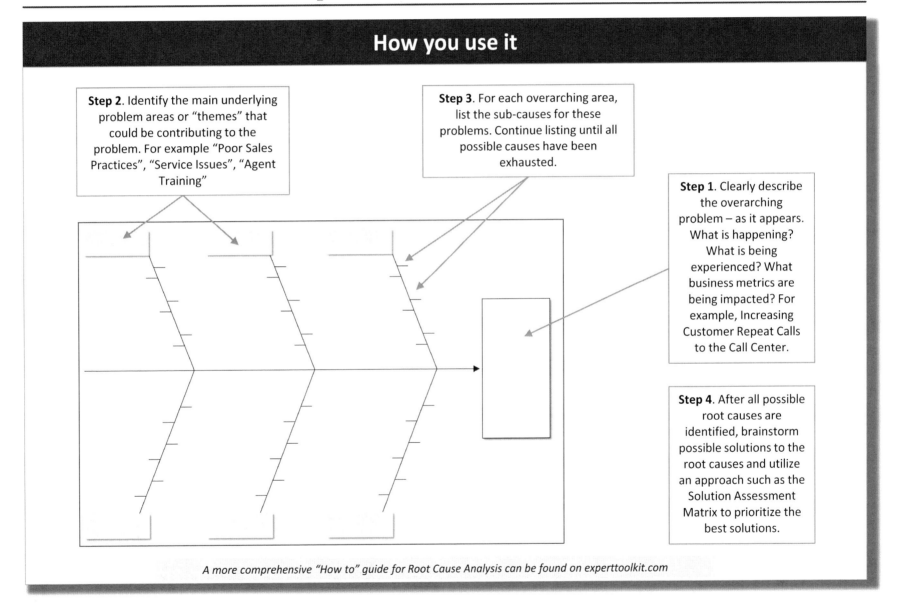

Step 2. Identify the main underlying problem areas or "themes" that could be contributing to the problem. For example "Poor Sales Practices", "Service Issues", "Agent Training"

Step 3. For each overarching area, list the sub-causes for these problems. Continue listing until all possible causes have been exhausted.

Step 1. Clearly describe the overarching problem – as it appears. What is happening? What is being experienced? What business metrics are being impacted? For example, Increasing Customer Repeat Calls to the Call Center.

Step 4. After all possible root causes are identified, brainstorm possible solutions to the root causes and utilize an approach such as the Solution Assessment Matrix to prioritize the best solutions.

A more comprehensive "How to" guide for Root Cause Analysis can be found on experttoolkit.com

Root Cause Analysis – Template

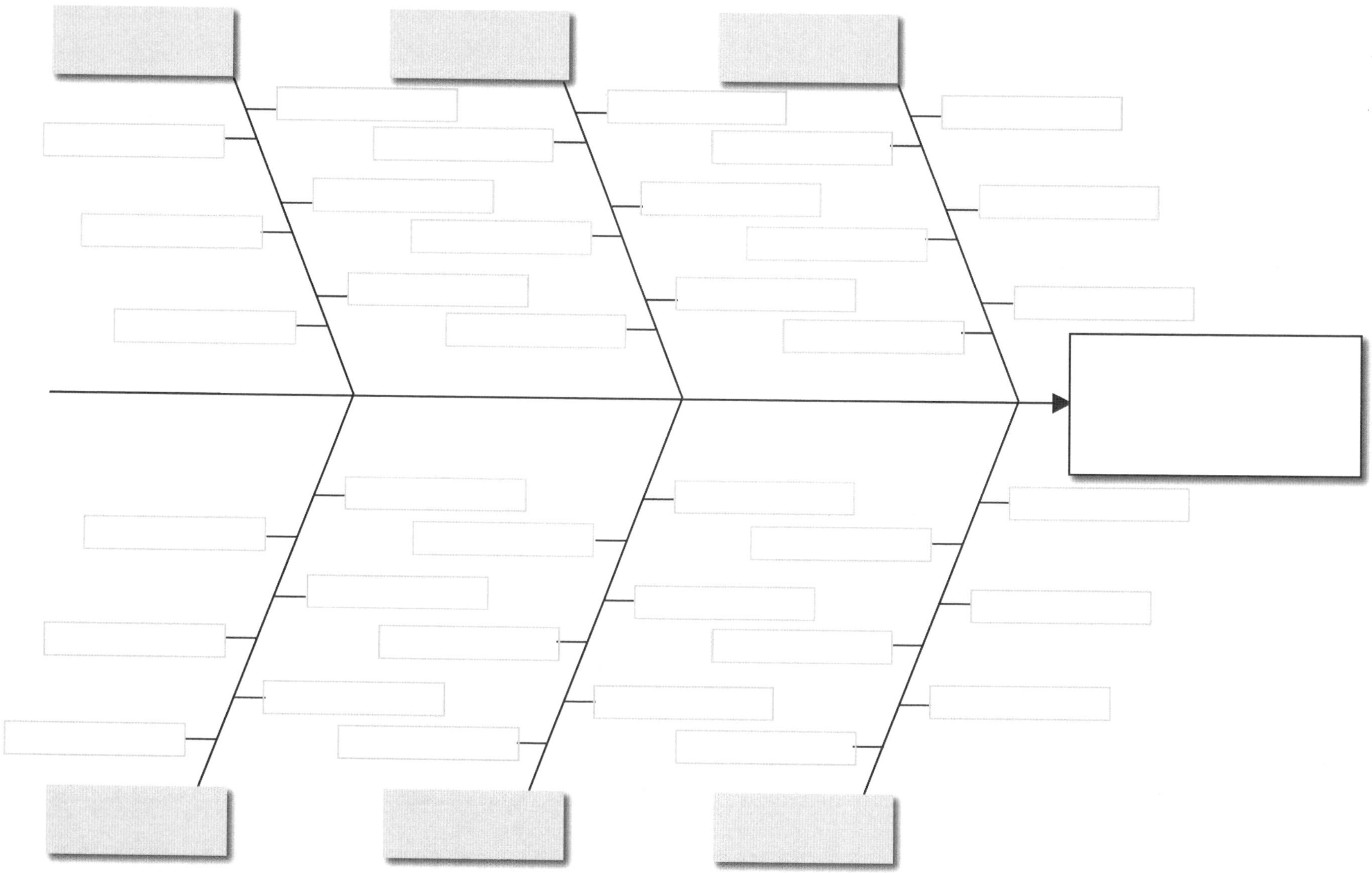

EXPERT TOOLKIT
—— MAKE A GREATER IMPACT ——

SIPOC Template

A useful tool for understanding the boundaries, actors
and inputs that make up a customer-facing process

SIPOC – Overview

What is it

SIPOC stands for "Suppliers, Inputs, Process, Outputs, Customers". It is a fairly simple method for capturing and laying out the critical elements, actors, inputs and steps associated with delivering value to a customer through an end-to-end business process. It is primarily used for process understanding, scoping and high level problem diagnosis.

When to use it

SIPOC is best used in situations where a process or value chain is utilized to deliver customer value – and it is performing sub-optimally or is poorly understood by key stakeholders. It is especially useful in a group setting (such as a workshop) for establishing a baseline level of understanding for a complex process or value chain that involves multiple actors and steps to deliver an outcome to a customer. It is also a useful tool for clarifying scope boundaries, and roles and responsibilities across a complex process.

Why use it

SIPOC can be used to bring understanding and clarity to a value chain that takes "raw ingredients" from suppliers and produces outputs and value for a customer. Having a clear and common understanding of key process elements and boundaries is a good starting point for more comprehensive process analysis and value chain diagnosis utilizing more analytical methods.

SIPOC – Method

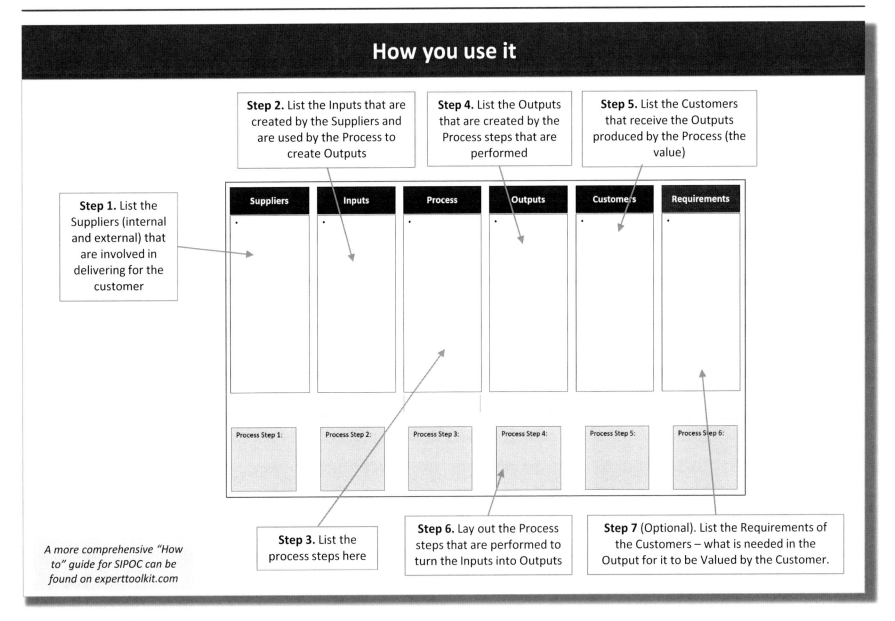

Step 1. List the Suppliers (internal and external) that are involved in delivering for the customer

Step 2. List the Inputs that are created by the Suppliers and are used by the Process to create Outputs

Step 4. List the Outputs that are created by the Process steps that are performed

Step 5. List the Customers that receive the Outputs produced by the Process (the value)

Suppliers	Inputs	Process	Outputs	Customers	Requirements
Process Step 1:	Process Step 2:	Process Step 3:	Process Step 4:	Process Step 5:	Process Step 6:

A more comprehensive "How to" guide for SIPOC can be found on experttoolkit.com

Step 3. List the process steps here

Step 6. Lay out the Process steps that are performed to turn the Inputs into Outputs

Step 7 (Optional). List the Requirements of the Customers – what is needed in the Output for it to be Valued by the Customer.

The Business Analysis Toolkit

SIPOC – Template

Suppliers	Inputs	Process	Outputs	Customers	Requirements
•	•	•	•	•	•

Process Step 1:	Process Step 2:	Process Step 3:	Process Step 4:	Process Step 5:	Process Step 6:

Solution Assessment Method

A proven approach for assessing the value and risk associated with potential business improvement solutions

Solution Assessment – Overview

What is it

The Solution Assessment Method is a proven approach for evaluating potential business improvement solutions and initiatives across a range of essential dimensions. The approach provides an objective lens when reviewing potential solutions that are identified to address business performance issues and their underlying root causes. The method is highly adaptable, easily customized to suit the specific application and accommodate different assessment criteria and weightings.

When to use it

The Solution Assessment Method is best suited once current state analysis has been conducted and a clear, accurate view of business performance issues, pain points are understood and potential solutions have been ideated. With the potential solutions that have been brainstormed or proposed, the Solution Assessment Method can be utilized to evaluate and prioritize the solutions with the aim of selecting the solutions which deliver the greatest business value with the least risk.

Why use it

The Solution Assessment Method is proven, flexible, adaptable and easy to use. It is intuitive for stakeholders involved in the process and for those who get to see and endorse the outcomes. The technique brings the right level of objectivity to what can be a political and subjective exercise, but without bogging down a business improvement program in overly complex and time wasting analysis.

Solution Assessment – Method

How you use it

Step 2. Allocate a score to the solution for its ability to resolve the root cause of the problem.

Step 3. Allocate a score to the solution for its likelihood to create any new problems.

Step 4. Allocate a score to the solution for the likelihood that business management will be receptive to its adoption.

Step 5. Allocate a score to the solution for the relative risk associated with its implementation.

Step 6. Allocate a score to the solution for the relative cost associated with its implementation.

Step 1. List the solutions that have been identified through the solution ideation process.

Step 7. Tabulate the scores for each solution by adding the values in columns 2 through 6.

Step 8. Rank the solutions by total score and select a finite number of the highest ranking solutions to proceed into more detailed evaluation and design.

Possible Solutions	Fixes the Root Cause	Creates New Problems	Management Receptivity	Risk & Feasibility	Cost	Total Score
	0 = Doesn't 1 = Limited 5 = Fully	0 = Significant 1 = Many 5 = None	0 = None 1 = Low 5 = High	0 = Not Feasible 1 = High Risk 5 = Low Risk	0 = Prohibitive 1 = Extreme 5 = Inexpensive	

Solution Assessment – Template

Possible Solutions	Fixes the Root Cause	Creates New Problems	Management Receptivity	Risk & Feasibility	Cost	Total Score
	0 = Doesn't 1 = Limited 5 = Fully	0 = Significant 1 = Many 5 = None	0 = None 1 = Low 5 = High	0 = Not Feasible 1 = High Risk 5 = Low Risk	0 = Prohibitive 1 = Extreme 5 = Inexpensive	

Solution Ideation & Ranking

A structured and proven approach for brainstorming and prioritizing business improvement initiatives

Solution Ideation & Ranking – Overview

What is it

Solution Ideation and Ranking is a proven, structured approach for brainstorming and prioritizing potential business improvement initiatives. The method utilizes a scoring system to measure the positive impact of potential business improvement projects against a set of targeted business metrics. The metrics should be chosen based on identified areas within the business where performance improvement is desired and the metrics are confirmed measures of associated performance improvement in the area.

When to use it

This method is useful when exploring potential initiatives to drive business improvement. It is best used after current state analysis has been performed and there is general agreement on what areas within the business are in need of performance improvement. The method is effective in workshop settings and the steps outlined on the following page can be used by a competent facilitator with an audience of stakeholders to arrive at a good outcome – a finite set of prioritized initiatives to assess further.

Why use it

The Solution Ideation and Ranking Method brings a level of structure and objectivity to what can sometimes be a subjective and emotional process – choosing which initiatives to prioritize. Led by a competent business analyst or facilitator, this technique is very useful at taking a long list of possible ideas and paring it down to a much shorter list of initiatives that can evaluated further. The method is also effective at soliciting executive endorsement for prioritization – given the structured process applied.

Solution Ideation & Ranking – Method

How you use it

Step 1: List the key areas of the business or process area where improvement is needed or being targeted.

Step 2: For each improvement area, identify and list the metrics that can be used to quantify a tangible improvement in the associated area. More than 1 metric can be listed for each area, list them separately (see example).

Step 5: Tally the scores for each project. Further assessment, scoping, design and implementation effort should then be allocated to the projects with the highest cumulative scores.

Step 3: Brainstorm the potential projects or initiatives that could be implemented in the business to drive improvement. Existing known project ideas can also be included in the assessment.

Step 4: For each project, allocate a score (1-5) representing the degree to which the project will have a positive impact on the KPIs identified. 0 or blank = none, 1 = minimal, 3 = moderate, 5 = significant.

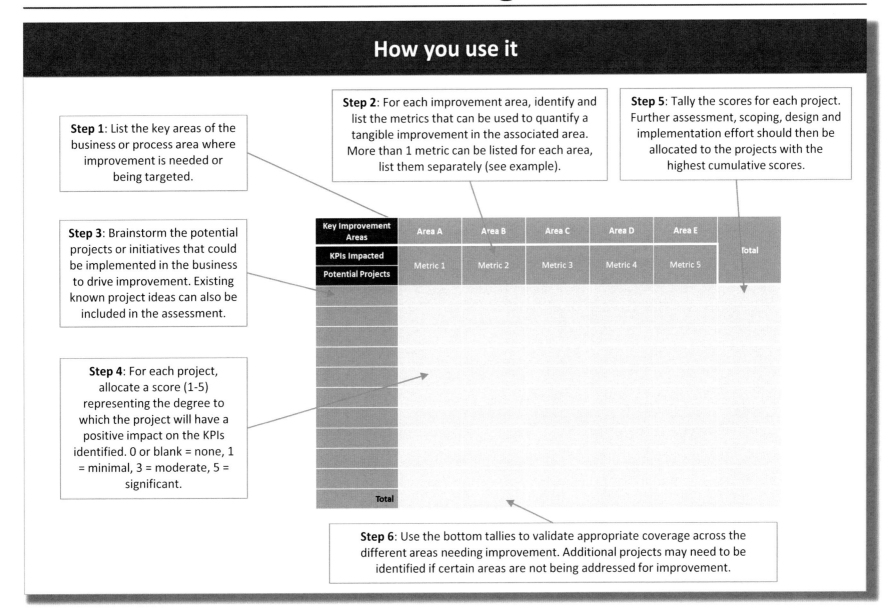

Key Improvement Areas	Area A	Area B	Area C	Area D	Area E	Total
KPIs Impacted / **Potential Projects**	Metric 1	Metric 2	Metric 3	Metric 4	Metric 5	
Total						

Step 6: Use the bottom tallies to validate appropriate coverage across the different areas needing improvement. Additional projects may need to be identified if certain areas are not being addressed for improvement.

Solution Ideation & Ranking – Template

Key Improvement Areas	Area A	Area B	Area C	Area D	Area E	Total
KPIs Impacted	Metric 1	Metric 2	Metric 3	Metric 4	Metric 5	
Potential Projects						
Total						

Solution Ideation & Ranking – Example

Key Improvement Areas	Growth	Customer Satisfaction		Costs		Total
KPIs Impacted						
Potential Projects	Revenue	NPS	Complaints	Time to Market	Headcount	
Project 1	1	2	2			5
Project 2		1	2	4		**7**
Project 3		3	1		3	**7**
Project 4		3		2		5
Project 5					4	4
Project 6	2		4		5	**11**
Project 7		1			5	6
Project 8	2		3			5
Project 9		3	2	4		**9**
Project 10		4		2		6
Total	5	17	14	12	17	

EXPERT TOOLKIT

—— MAKE A GREATER IMPACT ——

Swim Lane Process Map Template

A proven approach for laying out a process in order to provide clarity around accountabilities, steps, decisions and flows.

Swim Lane Process Map – Overview

What is it

The Swim Lane Process Map is a proven, logical and concise method for laying out a business or operational process in a way that provides clarity on core elements such as process actors, decision points, process steps and sequential flows. The approach and the format of the process map also accommodate additional notations and highlights to be added to draw attention to specific areas of interest, such as a process deficiencies, process volume data or opportunities for improvement.

When to use it

The Swim Lane Process Map is effective in two distinct business analysis situations. Firstly, it is effective at laying out a current state business process, highlighting key issues and socializing the process amongst stakeholders for awareness and agreement. Secondly, the same format is well suited for capturing a proposed future state – with emphasis given to recommended or proposed process changes and improvements to address identified gaps in the current state process.

Why use it

The Swim Lane Process Map is effective at capturing and conveying the core elements of any process being analyzed. It is simple, logical and minimizes the risk that important call outs within a process will get lost in a overly convoluted process diagram. A good process map should be readily understood by any business professional – and those with knowledge of the actual process should be able to confidently confirm that the process map represents reality. This tool enables this to occur.

Swim Lane Process Map – Method

Step 1. Name the overarching process being mapped and the sub-process being documented.

Step 2. List the roles that are involved in the process vertically down the page.

Step 3. Use boxes to indicate process steps, tasks or activities – ensuring they are positioned in the correct role lane and that the sequence flows from left to right.

Step 4. Use diamonds to indicate decision points involved in the process flow.

Step 5. Use ovals to indicate inputs or outputs that are involved in each process step.

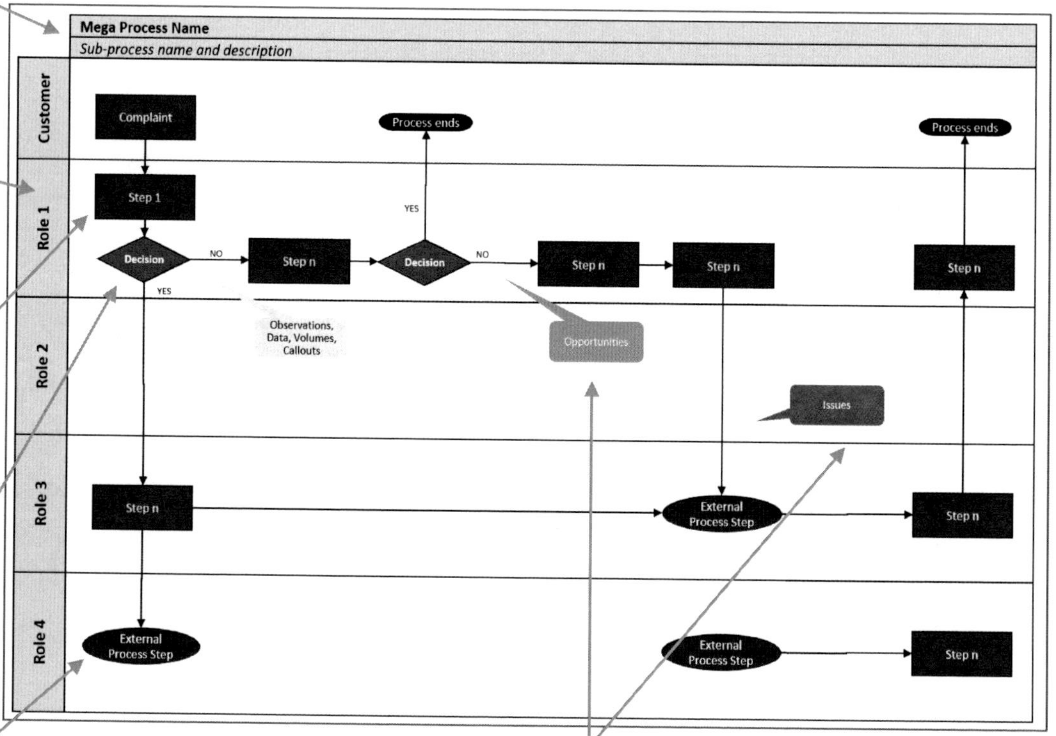

Step 6. Use call out boxes to indicate process issues, opportunities for improvement or other salient points.

Mega Process Name

Sub-process name and description

Customer	Complaint	
Role 1	Step 1	
	Decision — NO → Step n — Decision — NO → Step n → Step n	Process ends / Process ends / Step n
	YES	Observations, Data, Volumes, Callouts / Opportunities
Role 2		Issues
Role 3	Step n	External Process Step → Step n
Role 4	External Process Step	External Process Step → Step n

YES

Swim Lane Process Map – Template

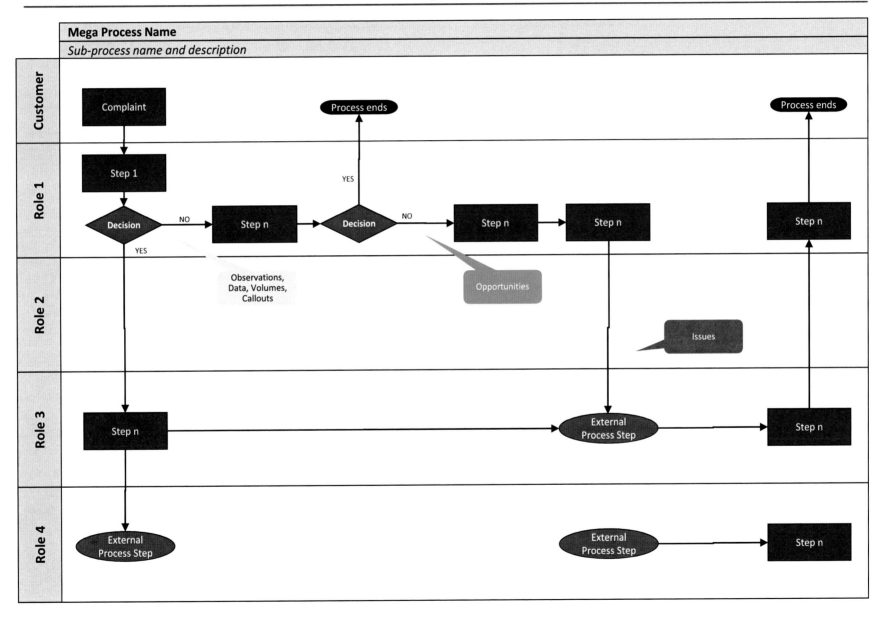

Notes

Notes

Notes

Notes

Notes

Disclaimer

- Descriptions and other related information in this document are provided only to illustrate the methods covered. You are fully responsible for the use of these methods where you see appropriate. Expert Toolkit assumes no responsibility for any losses incurred by you or third parties arising from the use of these methods or information.

- Expert Toolkit has used reasonable care in preparing the information included in this document, but Expert Toolkit does not warrant that such information is error free. Expert Toolkit assumes no liability whatsoever for any damages incurred by you resulting from errors in or omissions from the information included herein.

- Expert Toolkit does not assume any liability for infringement of patents, copyrights, or other intellectual property rights of third parties by or arising from the use of Expert Toolkit information described in this document. No license, express, implied or otherwise, is granted hereby under any patents, copyrights or other intellectual property rights of Expert Toolkit or others.

- This document may not be reproduced or duplicated in any form, in whole or in part, without prior written consent of Expert Toolkit.

- The document contains statements that are general in nature and do not constitute recommendations to the reader as to the content's suitability, applicability or appropriateness.